CAMBRIDGE INTRODUCTION TO WORLD HISTORY • TOPIC BOOK
GENERAL EDITOR • TREVOR CAIRNS

RUSSIA'S REVOLUTIONS

Tom Corfe

ACC NO : 15748-1
TITLE : RUSSIA'S REVOLUTIONS

AUTHOR : CORFE TOM

DDC(1) : 947.084

WITHDRAWN

CAMBRIDGE
Cambridge
New York
Melbourne Sydney

Published by the Press Syndicate of the University of Cambridge
The Pitt Building, Trumpington Street, Cambridge CB2 1RP
32 East 57th Street, New York, NY 10022, USA
10 Stamford Road, Oakleigh, Melbourne 3166, Australia

© Cambridge University Press 1989

First published 1989

Printed in Hong Kong by Wing King Tong

British Library cataloguing in publication data
  Corfe, Tom
  Russia's revolutions – (Cambridge introduction to world
  history)
  1. Soviet Union – History – 20th century
  2. Soviet Union – Politics and government – 20th century
  I. Title
  947.084   DK246

Library of Congress cataloguing in publication data
  Corfe, Tom, 1928-
  Russia's revolutions/Tom Corfe.
  64pp.   cm. – (Cambridge introduction to world history).
  1. Soviet Union – Politics and government – 20th century.
  2. Revolutions – Soviet Union – History – 20th century.   I. Title.
  II. Series.
  DK246.C67   1988.
  947.084 – dc19   87-13071   CIP

ISBN 0 521 31591 3

Front cover: *'Workers of the world unite! Long live the fifth anniversary of the great proletarian revolution!' A contemporary Soviet poster for the Fourth Congress of the Communist International.*

Back cover: *Red Square, Moscow. Long queues still form to see the embalmed body of Lenin which lies in a specially constructed stone mausoleum.*

Title page: *Lenin at the Finland Station, April 1917 (see p 29). The spirit of Russia's revolutions is captured in a scene often repeated by Soviet artists.*

Maps by Reg Piggott
Diagrams by Oxford Illustrators

Acknowledgements
Thanks are due to the following for permission to reproduce illustrations: Front cover, pp 10, 11, 12, 15, 16, 41, 44, 45, 47 (left) Novosti Press Agency; pp 6, 7, 14 The Mansell Collection; pp 8, 19, 23, 38, 56, 61 BBC Hulton Picture Library; pp 21, 27, 31, 35, 42, 57 David King; pp 34, 47 (right), 53, back cover Society for Cultural Relations with the USSR.

Contents

A note on dates
The 'February' and 'October' revolutions of 1917 took place, by Western reckoning, in March and November; only later did the USSR drop the old calendar. The modern calendar is used here.

ARCTIC OCEAN

GERMANY

Baltic Sea

FINLAND

POLAND

St Petersburg
(Petrograd 1914)
(Leningrad 1924)

Moscow

UKRAINE Ⓚ

Odessa
Ⓣ Donets
Coalfield

R Don

R Volga

Tsaritsyn
(Stalingrad 1925)
(Volgograd 1961)

Black Sea

GEORGIA
Ⓢ

TURKEY

Caspian Sea

KAZAKHSTAN

Ⓛ

Ural Mountains

Trans - Siberian Railway

R Ob

R Yenisei

R Lena

PACIFIC
OCEAN

SIBERIA

Irkutsk

MANCHURIA

Vladivostok

MONGOLIA

IRAN

AFGHANISTAN

CENTRAL ASIA

CHINA

Trotsky
was a Jew

About
90 small
nationalities

JEWS
GERMANS
GEORGIANS
TATARS
BELORUSSIANS

Stalin was
a Georgian

UZBEKS

UKRAINIANS

RUSSIANS

Peoples of the Soviet Union
(based on the 1979 census)

The Russian Empire and the Soviet Union

—— Boundary of Russian Empire in 1914

········ Soviet Union in 1985 where
boundary differs

ⓁⓉⓈⓀ Birthplaces of Lenin, Trotsky,
Stalin and Khruschev respectively

0 _____ 1500 km

0 _____ 1000 miles

The first decree of Russia's revolutionary government in October 1917 proclaimed peace. It appeared in next day's issue of Izvestia ('News'), the official paper of the All-Russian Congress of Soviets. "The Workers' and Peasants' Government," it begins, "proposes . . . a just, democratic peace."

№ 208.
Пятница,
27 октября 1917 г.

ИЗВѢСТІЯ

ЦѢНА:
въ Петроградѣ **15** коп.
на ст. жел. д. **18** коп.

Центральнаго Исполнительнаго Комитета
и ПЕТРОГРАДСКАГО СОВѢТА
РАБОЧИХЪ и СОЛДАТСКИХЪ ДЕПУТАТОВЪ.

Адресъ конторы: Литовка, Сайкинъ пер., д. № 6. Телефонъ № 218-41.
Адресъ редакціи: Смольный Институтъ, 2-й этажъ комната № 14½. Телефонъ № 38-89.

Декретъ о мирѣ,

принятый единогласно на засѣданіи Все-
россійскаго Съѣзда Совѣтовъ Рабочихъ,
Солдатскихъ и Крестьянскихъ Депутатовъ
26 октября 1917 г.

The 'Russian Revolution' usually means the Bolshevik seizure of power in 1917. Sometimes it is called the 'October Revolution'; though by the western calendar, which Russians only used later, it took place in November. The October Revolution began a new age, dividing peoples and politicians everywhere into admirers and opponents of the Russian way.

There were other Russian revolutions. What was once the Empire of the Romanov Tsars is an enormous country, one-sixth of the world's land. Before the coming of air travel it took many days, even months, to get from Siberian forests to Ukrainian farmlands, from Arctic tundra to the steppes and deserts of central Asia, from the frontiers of Germany to the shores of the Pacific. Only half of the Empire's millions were actually Russian, and today many national groups are linked in the Union of Soviet Socialist Republics. A country so vast and varied needs an energetic and powerful government, and from time to time revolutionary Russians – rulers, like Peter the Great, and would-be rulers – have tried to jolt all the peoples into a new way of life. In the twentieth century there have been three such revolutions. One, like Peter's, came from above. Two came from below, when people with fervent ideals overthrew their rulers. But the story starts in 1905 with a 'dress rehearsal'.

1 1905: the revolution that failed

'Bloody Sunday'. The shooting of unarmed strikers by the
Tsar's troops caused widespread horror, and artists who never
saw it produced highly dramatic pictures.

Bloody Sunday: St Petersburg, January 1905

One bleak Sunday the factory workers of Russia's capital city, with their families, set off through the snow. Perhaps 200,000 in all, they moved steadily in processions towards the Emperor's Winter Palace, singing hymns, carrying crosses and religious pictures. They were on strike against their employers, and they wanted the Emperor, their 'Little Father', to help.

The Emperor was not there. He was 24 kilometres (15 miles) away at his country estate, Tsarskoe Selo. Instead, there were soldiers, whose commander was worried by these enormous crowds. There had been trouble in the city of late – strikes, disorders and murders.

Cossack horsemen rode into the crowds to break them up, hitting out roughly with their sabres. In the chaos people began to scream, milling round to escape. Some stood to hit back at the soldiers. Then the infantry opened fire on the surging masses. In all the shooting, slashing and stampeding perhaps a thousand men, women and children were injured or killed.

'Bloody Sunday' was the start of a year of strikes, riots, murders and executions all over Russia. What had been an argument with employers turned into a bitter conflict between the Russians and their rulers. 'The present Tsar,' wrote an American onlooker, 'will never again be safe in the midst of his people.'

Tsar and Tsarism

Tsar Nicholas II, 'Autocrat (or absolute ruler) of All the Russias', was a gentle, well-meaning man, devoted to his family. Nicholas thought he knew how to govern Russia, but he was neither clever nor ruthless enough – fit only to live in a country house and grow turnips, according to his cousin, Kaiser William II. His father, the burly, unimaginative Alexander III had shown him how to rule, and his tutor had explained many times. The Tsar must be father to all his people, whatever their race or class; benevolent and all-seeing, stern and just. God would guide him; to no one else was he responsible, to no other advice need he listen. He alone appointed and dismissed ministers, and he might heed their words or ignore them. His governors controlled the fifty

Nicholas and Alexandra wearing 17th-century costume. In 1913 there were splendid celebrations of three hundred years of Romanov rule. Tsar and Tsarina are here dressed like their ancestors before the sweeping reforms of Peter the Great did away with traditional costume.

provinces of European Russia, many the size of small countries. Other nations, like the democracies of western Europe, might prefer elections, parliaments, a cabinet led by a prime minister, an opposition, a free press. Such things would simply not work in Russia, with scores of different races and millions of illiterate peasants. Only common loyalty to the Tsar held

The assassination of Alexander II in March, 1881. The Tsar Liberator was killed by Narodnaia Volia *conspirators led by a determined young woman on the very day when he had approved new reforms. Their bombs killed several of his escort and some of the crowd as well.*

the peoples of his Empire together, and nothing must come between them. For the peasants in particular, five-sixths of all his subjects, the Tsar was 'Little Father', judge and law-giver.

There was one tragic example of what could happen if a Tsar tried to bring in western liberal ideas before Russia was ready. In 1861 Nicholas's grandfather, Alexander II, had freed millions of serfs on the estates of Russia's great land-owners. Peasants were no longer the property of their masters, to be bought and sold like cattle. They could move freely, marry freely and farm for themselves. Three years later Alexander set up *zemstvos*, elected local councils, to take charge of roads, bridges, health care and schools. Landowners who had once been responsible for these matters found themselves working alongside their former serfs in the zemstvo.

These changes were welcomed by progressively minded Russians, educated in western ideas, as a step towards free-dom and democracy. Yet things were no easier for the peasants, left with too little land, too many debts, and the burden of repaying the government over forty years for the land it had bought for them from the landowners. Moreover, the land was given not to each peasant personally, but to the village community, the *mir*; and the mir's restrictions and regulations were often as bad as the landowner's had been.

As for the zemstvos, they gave many people a chance to complain. Landowners who had lost their serfs led a chorus of objections to Alexander II's interference. On the other hand 'liberals' or 'progressives' wanted Russia transformed into a constitutional monarchy on the western pattern. By 1881 Alexander was ready for a step further in this direction; the zemstvos all over Russia were to elect delegates to advise his Council of State. At last Russia would have some sort of national assembly.

Other critics went further. Many were students, young idealists, who wanted a new socialist form of society with equality and land for all. Feeling passionate sympathy for the peasants and believing in the common people, they came to be called *Narodniks*, or Populists. At first the Narodniks urged the peasants to demand more of the Tsar. When that failed, some turned to violence. Calling themselves *Narodnaia Volia*, the People's Will, they set out to destroy the Tsar and his government. In 1881 their bombs blew the 'Tsar Liberator' to pieces in a St Petersburg street. The future Nicholas II was not quite thirteen when his grandfather was murdered.

Alexander III was determined not to repeat his father's mistakes. He declared,

> The voice of God commands Us to stand resolutely by the task of governing . . . with faith in the strength and truth of autocratic power, which we have been called to confirm and protect for the good of the people.

But strengthening autocracy meant adding to the hosts of bureaucrats – inspectors, clerks, officials, uniformed busybodies who kept close watch on everyone. The police especially were given wide powers. They could interfere whenever they scented trouble, censor newspapers, check on people's movements, and issue or withdraw the passports that everyone had to carry. Spies and informers kept the police well supplied with news of troublemakers; and sometimes agents stirred up disorder just to catch the ringleaders. Terrorists were hunted down by the *Okhrana*, the new political police. Five of those who had planned Alexander II's murder were publicly hanged, though the death penalty was rare in Tsarist Russia. Many others were exiled to Siberia or fled abroad.

Alexander III gave more power to provincial governors. If danger threatened they might set up military rule, dismiss officials or whole zemstvos, close colleges and newspapers. The peasants' share in zemstvo elections was reduced. Government officials took over some zemstvo jobs. 'Land Captains', usually local landowners, were placed in charge of each village. Enterprising peasants found it more difficult than ever to break from the mir and work for themselves.

Interfering officials and their slow, bureaucratic methods were a nuisance, but peasants were resigned to it, or too busy to complain. Most remained simple, loyal subjects, proud to be Russian. Some ministers and provincial governors sought to strengthen and use that pride. When discontent arose, they directed it against non-Russians, both inside and outside the Empire. Turks, English, Austrians and Japanese were blamed as foreign enemies, while Finns, Poles, Georgians and Jews were labelled as disloyal subjects, slow to accept Russian language, Russian customs and Russian Orthodox Christianity. The Jews in particular were a main target; their loyalty seemed to be to their own faith and people rather than to Russia, their habits were deliberately different, and they appeared to make money at the expense of honest Russian peasants. Plehve, the Tsar's principal police official, encouraged *pogroms*, when local people, sometimes with government troops to help, drove Jews from their homes, pillaged and murdered them.

This was the system that Nicholas II inherited, and he sought to follow his father's example. Police rule under Plehve (who soon became Minister of the Interior) continued; yet in 1905 it failed to prevent Bloody Sunday. In one way police activities even helped to cause it. Keen to have a hand in everything, they had actually taken to organising trade unions for discontented workers. Thus, the police hoped to help workers satisfy their needs without disorder, to control the direction their anger took, or perhaps to play off workers against employers so that the Tsar and his ministers could step in to heal the breach. So it came about that Father Gapon, the handsome young priest who led the workers' appeal to the Tsar on Bloody Sunday, was in fact an Okhrana agent, an idealist who hoped to see a stronger, happier autocracy emerge from the workers' discontent. But the police network was tangled into a hopeless knot, and the result was a massacre.

Industry and the workers

The revolutionary upheavals of 1905 affected people of all classes, but factory workers in particular began strikes, demonstrations and street battles. Those who marched on Bloody Sunday came from the giant Putilov plant, producing steel, locomotives and armaments. By October, strikes had spread widely; railways, factories and even whole towns came to a standstill. Workers in St Petersburg and some other towns chose their own councils, or *soviets*, to voice their demands. From time to time, throughout Russian history, there had been outbreaks of violence among the peasants, but strikes of industrial workers were something new. Russia's first large-scale strike in 1896 had demanded a cut in textile workers' thirteen-hour day; each year since, more days' work had been lost through strikes.

Most of this unrest resulted from Russia's strenuous efforts to catch up with the industrialised nations in the west. The

The Putilov Works, St Petersburg, with some of their many thousand workers.

Crimean War defeat of 1854–6 had revealed the dangers of falling behind western Europe, and Alexander II promptly started Russia on the path to industrial revolution. If ending serfdom was his most spectacular move towards modern standards, encouraging new industries was part of the same process. Above all, the building of railways began in earnest. Railways would close the vast distances that separated towns and regions, linking factories to raw materials and markets. St Petersburg's iron-using industries, for example, were now linked by rail to the Donets coalfield in the south. Before long

400,000 Russians were employed in railway-building, and the demand for rails and locomotives stimulated the growth of blast furnaces, factories and mines. But still Britain, Germany and the USA were well in front and advancing even faster, so more efforts were needed.

Really rapid growth began around 1890, and Sergei Witte played a key part. Alexander III placed him in charge of railways in 1889, and made him Finance Minister three years later. Witte had grown up in the railway industry; he was practical, forceful and efficient, but rude and boastful. Determined to modernise the country, he believed it could be done only by using the autocratic powers of the Tsar. In his way Witte was a revolutionary like Peter the Great, or like Stalin in later years, though he did not hold supreme power himself. He encouraged western capitalists to build mining enterprises and industrial plants, while he poured government money (much of it borrowed abroad) into building railways where no private company could afford the cost or risk. Most spectacular of all was the Trans-Siberian Railway, started in 1891 and mostly built over the next eight years. Stretching more than 6,000 kilometres (3,750 miles) from the Ural Mountains to the Pacific, the longest railway in the world, it crossed terrain of frightful difficulty to reach the two-thirds of the Empire that other transport had barely touched.

Witte wanted Russia to stop being simply a market for richer nations' manufactures, selling in return only raw materials produced by unskilled labour. He wrote: 'Russia is a politically independent and mighty power; it need not and must not pay tribute for ever to the economically more advanced states.' So he started technical colleges to turn out skilled workers, he organised industrial exhibitions to spread new ideas, and he set up banks to finance industrial growth. He taxed imported goods heavily to protect Russia's own manufactures.

Length of railways and industrial output both doubled during Witte's time in office. Output rose by 8 or 9 per cent each

Relative industrial production

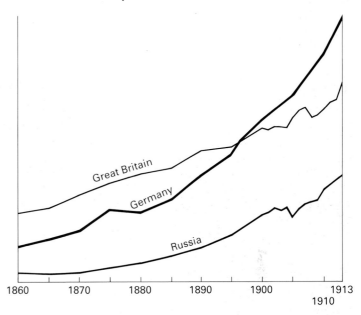

Russia's industrial production rose rapidly from 1890, despite a check in 1905. But it remained far behind the great industrial countries.

year. Large-scale, well-equipped industries using the most modern techniques developed, and Russia joined the half-dozen leading industrial nations. With vast supplies of labour and raw materials Russia would soon, it seemed, surpass most of them.

But the spread of change brought problems. Some new industries, lacking firm roots, collapsed in a slump at the start of the new century. Witte's tariff duties forced up prices so that Russians could not afford foreign goods such as machinery that might have improved agricultural production. The new railways cost 3,000 million roubles, and the government also subsidised many industrial firms and spent heavily on training and bank loans. To pay for all this, taxes became heavier; most were indirect, falling on goods rather than personal wealth, hitting the needy harder than the rich. Witte argued that this temporary sacrifice would bring universal prosperity in the future.

The industrial workers lived in harsh conditions. They

Rail-laying in 1899 on the central stretch of the Trans-Siberian Railway near Krasnoyarsk, where it crossed the Yenisei River.

11

Peasants at the well in a village typical of south-east Russia, not far from the Volga River.

crowded into ramshackle shanty towns that shot up in new industrial regions like the great Donets coalfield, or around the fringes of St Petersburg. More labourers flocked from impoverished and overcrowded villages in search of a new life. Life turned out to be no better; but, crowded in their thousands, it was easier for the discontented workers to organise protest and act together.

Peasant farmers

Life in the villages was getting even harder. Farming in Russia was primitive, less than half as productive as in the west. The mirs kept to old-fashioned methods, sharing out land in scattered strips and discouraging those who wished for change. The population was growing rapidly, so more villagers each year wanted a share. Many peasants lived in filthy, pest-ridden huts of wood or mud. Often they could not afford a horse to help with the ploughing. They were getting less money for their grain, as wheat from the North American prairies was flooding world markets and bringing down prices. From time to time exceptionally bad harvests caused famine; in 1891–2 thousands died of starvation.

Sometimes there were outbursts of resentment and violence; in 1901 and 1902, for example, there were widespread riots in the rich southern provinces. Yet most peasants worked on steadily. They believed there was no alternative to hardship; it was God's will, and the Tsar loved his peasants, even if he was far off. The rise of industry offered some a new hope.

In one of the poorest villages lived Sergei Khrushchev. Each winter he travelled 500 kilometres (310 miles) to work in the booming Donets coalfield. Even so, he never saved enough to buy himself a horse. In the end he decided to move his whole family out for good. His son, Nikita, who had been a village herdboy, started work at 'a factory owned by Germans, at pits owned by Frenchmen, and at a chemical plant owned by Belgians'. Later he remembered that 'all they wanted was the most work for the least money'. Further to the south, in Georgia, Vissarion Djugashvili, born a serf, tried to set up as a shoemaker. He failed, and instead left his wife and son to work in a shoe factory in Tiflis.

David Bronstein was more successful, despite the prejudice he faced as a Jew. He bought a tiny holding in sparsely-populated steppeland north of the Black Sea; over the years hard work and shrewdness turned it into a sizeable farm. He had barns filled with wheat, cowsheds, pigsties, a machine shop, labourers' quarters; his mill ground all the grain for miles around. In the end he replaced the leaky mud farmhouse with a fine brick dwelling, and sent his son Lev (or Leon) to university.

There were other ways of advancement for those who left the village. Russia's army, unlike those of Germany and Britain, drew many of its officers from the poorest classes; two-fifths of them came from the peasantry. Others joined the ever-growing police force. Some tried the Church. Only its lower ranks were open to those who did not give up the world altogether to become monks, but even the life of a village priest offered security and broader interests. Vissarion Djugashvili's widow sent her son to train as a priest, but Joseph came to hate his teachers and the Church he was intended to serve.

Finally, as a way ahead, there was the all-embracing civil service. A job there meant respectability and perhaps wealth.

The growth of Russia's population

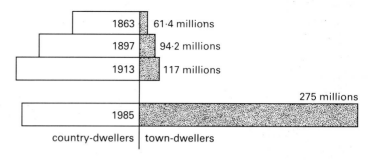

Ilya Ulyanov, son of a serf who had bought his freedom and become a tailor, went to university to be a teacher. When Alexander II expanded the school system in the 1860s, Ilya became first an inspector and then director of education for the province of Simbirsk. He was hard-working and enterprising, doing much to improve schools. He was rewarded by a rank of nobility and the right to be addressed as 'Excellency'.

The successful director's two sons became revolutionaries. So did the sons of Sergei Khrushchev, Djugashvili and Bronstein.

Revolutionaries and reformers

It needed leadership to turn discontent, strikes and riots into revolution, and from the time of Alexander II would-be leaders had been appearing. Educated people, writers and teachers – the *intelligentsia* – tried to show Russians what was wrong with Tsarism and how it might be changed.

Elementary education was spreading slowly downwards through Russian society, thanks especially to the reforms of Alexander II and the efforts of men like Ilya Ulyanov. By the end of the century about half of Russia's peasants were getting some kind of schooling; even poor families like the Khrushchevs and Djugashvilis sent their children to the village school.

But the new leaders came from the universities, not the elementary schools. University students usually came from well-off families, like those of the top civil servant, Ulyanov, or the prosperous farmer, Bronstein. Sometimes they followed their fathers' professions; but many, finding no comfortable place in the imperial bureaucracy, turned to complaining about Russia's misfortunes and criticising the Tsarist government. Lev Bronstein had no sooner arrived at Odessa University in 1897 than he set about planning a 'Southern Russian Workers' Union'; he was quickly arrested and sent off to Siberia to calm down. Even the police crack-down after 1881 could not stop students plotting, though their schemes never got far. One plan to assassinate Alexander III was uncovered at St Petersburg University in 1887. Five of the plotters, refusing to ask for mercy, were hanged. One was Alexander Ulyanov, whose father had recently died.

Under Nicholas II, as unrest grew among workers and peasants, the Narodnik movement revived. In 1901 it re-formed as a new political organisation, the Socialist Revolutionary Party. The Socialist Revolutionaries, SRs as they were generally known, placed their faith in Russia's peasant masses. If only Tsarist autocracy were ended, they thought, then the country people, left with no focus for simple-minded loyalty, would wake up and turn towards peasant socialism. Some SRs determined to hasten this by destroying the Tsar's ministers one by one. These extremists were few, but their murder campaign was the most deadly threat to Tsarism.

Danger in another form came from the Liberals, who hoped to end absolutism by peaceful means. They were more numerous and more outspoken with their own newspaper called *Liberation*, smuggled into Russia from Germany. Liberals in the zemstvos constantly called for reform. In 1903 they formed an underground political party, the 'Union of Liberation', to demand a Constitution for Russia in which the Tsar would cease to be an autocrat and would rule with a parliament. The Union's principal leader was a professor of history, Paul Miliukov.

Marxists

There was another anti-Tsarist group, so small, so remote and argumentative that it did not concern the government much. These were Social Democrats, who accepted the ideas of the German revolutionary thinker, Karl Marx. The Marxists pointed out that the peasants were no longer the only workers in Russia. They claimed that the country was at last passing from its 'feudal stage' of rule by landowner and autocrat, and would soon be run by industrial capitalists. Marx had argued that capitalism naturally produced a class of wage-earning

Karl Marx (1818–1883) started as a German revolutionary but spent most of his life in London as a scholar. His books, articles and letters dissected the injustices of capitalist society.

factory workers, a 'proletariat'. In time the proletariat would become strong enough to supplant the capitalists, creating a workers' state. In a socialist system all would be rewarded justly for their labour, and no one would profit from exploiting others. It would become possible to build an ideal 'communist' society, where everyone would work for the good of the community, and all needs would be met by the community.

This vision inspired both Russian exiles in Switzerland and secret groups at universities inside Russia. Unlike the SRs, the Marxists thought that factory workers would make better revolutionaries than peasants, but they saw no need for guns and bombs to destroy a government that would collapse anyway when capitalism did. The revolution was sure to come, so they could talk about Marx's ideas without having to do anything.

But by 1895 two young Marxists at St Petersburg had become impatient, and tried to speed change by organising trade union activities. They were Julius Tsederbaum, from a well-off Jewish family, who called himself Martov; and Vladimir Ulyanov, Alexander's younger brother, who later used the name Lenin. They wanted Marxists to educate workers in readiness for the coming revolution. The two were arrested, tried, and sent to Siberia for a few years. Their exile was not hard; Lenin (whose mother had influence in high places) lived comfortably, and continued his revolutionary activities.

In 1898 other Marxists met secretly at Minsk to form the Russian Social Democratic Labour Party. As the Okhrana knew all about the 'secret' meeting and promptly arrested most members, the new party got off to a shaky start. But two years later, when Lenin came back from Siberia, the Social Democrats were able to start their own newspaper. *Iskra* it was called, 'the Spark' which they hoped would start a mighty fire. Lenin also published his own ideas on how the party might hasten revolution; his booklet, *What is to be Done?* was passed around secretly throughout the Empire. Even in Georgia young Djugashvili, recently expelled from college, read it and started a group to support Lenin.

In 1903 the Social Democrats held a congress, safely outside Russia. Fifty-seven delegates made their way to Bussels, moving to London when asked to leave by the Belgian police. There they argued hotly about just how to behave when the revolution eventually came. Lenin emerged as the most fiercely determined of them all, demanding time and again that the Party seize any and every opportunity to hurry history along. The Party must teach, organise and lead the workers in disrupting the state and taking power; since the workers themselves had not read Marx and would not know how to run a socialist state, the Party must provide guidance and leadership. Lenin's fierce intolerance frightened many delegates. Others were impressed by his passionate arguments and unshakeable certainty. His determination split the infant party; those following Lenin called themselves *Bolsheviks*, the 'larger group'. The rest, following Martov, wanted co-operation with other parties seeking changes and progress. They were henceforth the *Mensheviks*.

The Japanese War 1904–5

A few quarrelling talkers in a foreign land mattered little to the Tsar's ministers. They were much more worried by the SR assassinations and the propaganda of the Liberals. The interior minister Plehve remarked in 1904 that 'What we need to hold Russia back from revolution is a small, victorious war.' Within months war came, but it was far from victorious.

Russia's expansion to the shores of the Pacific had brought her face to face with the rising empire of Japan. War seemed

Vladimir Ilyich Ulyanov, later Lenin (1870–1924), as a student in 1891.

Officers and men of a Siberian rifle brigade beside rail flat-cars carrying field artillery on the Trans-Siberian Railway near Lake Baikal, 1904.

likely, but when it came the Japanese took Russia by surprise. They destroyed Russia's Far East fleet, and defeated the Russian army in Manchuria, at the end of the long, slow Trans-Siberian Railway.

Plehve did not see the worst disasters, for he was killed by a terrorist bomb in the summer of 1904. Dismal tales from the Far East infuriated people who already disliked the government. That November Liberal members from all the zemstvos gathered in St Petersburg for a great congress. They spoke out more boldly than ever before, demanding democratic reform to give Russia a constitution, and their demands were taken up in cities, factories and villages. When, a few weeks later, in

January 1905, St Petersburg workers began a major strike, the authorities feared that it might well boil over into serious riots, or even revolution. The workers' appeal to the Tsar asked for an eight-hour day and better wages; but it also asked for freedom from corrupt and oppressive officials, the right to discuss taxes and the right to form trade unions:

> The people must be represented in control of the country's affairs . . . Let all be free and equal . . . let the election of members to the Constituent Assembly [to prepare a new constitution] take place in conditions of universal, secret and equal suffrage.

Revolution was in the air, and this alarmed the military commanders. But their attempt to disperse what they saw as a dangerous crowd on Bloody Sunday produced just the effect the government most dreaded.

The October Manifesto

As 1905 went on it seemed that the Tsar's government was collapsing. In May came a final naval disaster: Russia's Baltic fleet sailed halfway round the world to meet the Japanese in battle at Tsushima, and was utterly destroyed. Russia admitted defeat and made peace.

Near the Black Sea port of Odessa, aboard those Russian warships still left, mutiny was close. The *Potemkin*'s crew seized the ship in June, murdered their officers, and eventually sailed off to a foreign port. Odessa itself was briefly in the hands of revolutionaries.

In the St Petersburg Soviet, representatives gathered from the city's factories and revolutionary groups. Here Social Democrat members launched bitter attacks on the Tsar, demanding a workers' government; their leader was the fiery young Lev Bronstein, who now called himself Trotsky. Strikes and rural disorder spread throughout the summer. Soon, it

Battleship Potemkin. *In 1905 its sailors mutinied. Twenty years later the director Sergei Eisenstein made an exciting film about their heroic stand against bad conditions and harsh officers; it was splendid propaganda for the new Soviet government.*

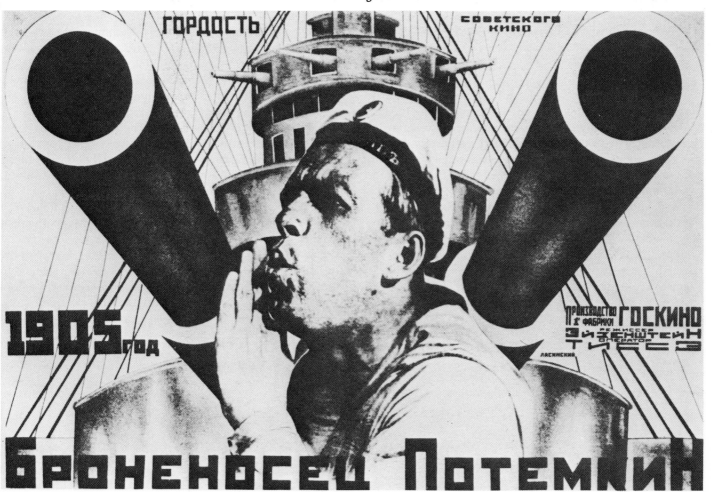

17

seemed, all work would stop. Throughout Russia people looked forward to changes that would make life happier.

The Tsar gave way, step by step. In March he promised to summon an Imperial *Duma*, an assembly, to advise him. In August he repeated his promise, and arranged for elections. When that did not stop the spread of unrest he went for advice to Witte, whom he had dismissed two years before. Witte advised both firmness and a generous offer to please the government's critics. In October the Tsar duly issued to his excited people the Manifesto that Witte had prepared:

> The rioting and agitation in . . . Our Empire fills Our heart with great and deep grief . . . We grant . . . the right of free citizenship, based on . . . freedom of person, conscience, assembly and union . . . We include in the work of the Duma those classes . . . that have been until now entirely deprived of the right to vote . . . No law shall go into force without its confirmation by the State Duma.

The October Manifesto implied that Russia would be ruled by elected assembly, prime minister and cabinet, as western countries were. Some of the Tsar's opponents welcomed it enthusiastically. For the Octobrists, supporters of the manifesto, the new Duma gave promise of freedom and progress; they were keen to make it work. Others, such as the Liberal Paul Miliukov and his supporters (known as Constitutional Democrats or Kadets), hoped that further changes would give Duma and electors greater power; but they too were ready to work through the Duma.

Others, like the SRs and Social Democrats, were not satisfied. They feared that the Manifesto was a trick of the Tsar's to gain time and rally his forces. But they disagreed on what to do next; and meanwhile starving workers desperately needed regular work and wages.

The Tsar made Witte his first prime minister, and Witte sensed that most people now wanted order restored. He used the police and army effectively. He encouraged loyal landowners and priests to raise gangs of volunteers, the 'Black Hundreds', to take action against those suspected of planning revolutionary violence. The Black Hundreds attacked students, intellectuals, strike leaders, and Jews. Witte regained control of trouble centres like Odessa, and he arrested most members of the St Petersburg Soviet.

The Social Democrats and SRs made one serious attempt to hit back. In December they called a general strike in Moscow that developed into an armed rising of some 2,000 workers. As troops marched in, the rebels met them at street barricades. But in ten days of fighting the Moscow rising was crushed. 1905, year of surging hopes, ended as bloodily as it had begun.

In remoter parts of the Empire, strikes and disorders went on. But now military courts were busy. Provincial governors restored order, with the army behind them. Some 4,000 people were executed and thousands more sent to imprisonment or exile. The revolution was stamped out.

1905 left a very different Russia. The Tsar still believed that he was an autocrat, with absolute power to care for Russia, under God's guidance. Yet he had accepted a constitution, a parliament and a prime minister. His subjects, if they wished, might now speak out against his policies and even block his laws. If the reformers worked wisely they might in time make Russia a democracy, where the laws of an elected parliament would replace the Tsar's decrees.

But many of his people no longer trusted the Tsar. Nor did the Tsar trust his people – or, rather, those who claimed to speak for them in his Duma. So the new Russia was born in an atmosphere of mutual suspicion and distrust.

2 March 1917: the end of Tsarism

Twelve years after Bloody Sunday, in March 1917, Nicholas II abdicated and the Russian Empire came to a dramatic end.

Often during those twelve years people had expected such a revolution to overthrow the Tsar. At other times it had seemed as if he might regain full autocratic power. Or perhaps Russia would progress steadily towards parliamentary monarchy. This is what many of the urban middle classes, lawyers, shopowners, teachers and journalists hoped.

Between 1905 and 1917 the violence lingered on, but revolutionary hopes faded. SR terrorists still pursued their assassination campaign; about 4,000 Tsarist officials and local magistrates fell victim to them in 1906. Peasants in the Baltic lands were still attacking landlords. Small 'fighting squads' of Social Democrats, Lenin's supporters, were active; in the Caucasus Joseph Djugashvili, calling himself 'Koba' after a legendary Georgian 'Robin Hood', organised a squad, and his murderous bank raids gathered roubles for Party funds. But the Tsar's troops and police hunted down such enemies of peace and order. 'Terror must be met by terror,' wrote the Tsar, and slowly law and authority returned. 'The peace of the grave', some called it.

Russia, though, was changing. Both Russians and foreigners wondered if a new, successful Empire might emerge from the troubles that had nearly destroyed the old. Historians still disagree over whether it could have, and why it never did.

The State Duma meeting in the Tauride Palace. Members sat in the lecture-theatre arrangement favoured by most western assemblies, rather than the parliamentary pattern where government party and opposition face each other. Members or ministers addressing the Duma spoke from the rostrum, with the Tsar's portrait behind them.

The Duma and its problems

Certainly the elected representatives from all over the Empire who met at the first Duma in the Tauride, one of St Petersburg's splendid palaces, were full of enthusiasm. They hoped to create a new age, working like a British parliament to give Russia the good laws it needed. There was to be equality for all, freedom of the press, and the right to strike.

But even as the Duma gathered in the spring of 1906 the Tsar announced new 'Fundamental Laws': 'To the Emperor of All the Russias belongs supreme autocratic power.' He could see only the danger that parliamentary government might disrupt and weaken his sprawling Empire of many peoples. So many different idealists, democrats and nationalists would bring only disputes and trouble where his people needed order and peace.

Representatives at the Duma included peasants, factory workers, lawyers, intelligentsia and landowners. Their ideas varied widely. Nationalists demanded more freedom for subject Poles, Ukrainians or Georgians, while Russians wanted them all to be 'good Russians'. There were SRs, Social Democrats, Kadets, and Octobrists all demanding reforms, and Tsarists who wanted no change. Out of five hundred members, about one hundred represented the peasants and workers; most of these were SRs, but since their party officially ignored the Duma, they called themselves *Trudoviks* ('Labourites').

Besides this multiplicity of parties and groups, there were other ways in which the Duma differed from Britain's parliament. The Duma could make no laws without the Tsar's consent, but the Tsar could make laws without the Duma when it was not assembled. Ministers were chosen by the Tsar, not the Duma, and appeared at the Tauride Palace only to announce the Tsar's wishes or to complain of Duma behaviour.

So members talked excitedly and argued fiercely, misunderstood one another, demanded all sorts of changes, and complained about the Tsar's advisers. The Tsar thought they were hopeless. After only two months he dismissed the first Duma.

A second Duma met early in 1907, but proved even more divided and quarrelsome. A Social Democrat member accused the Tsar's soldiers of massacre, and the Tsar's response was a second dismissal.

The Four Dumas: Changing Patterns of Membership

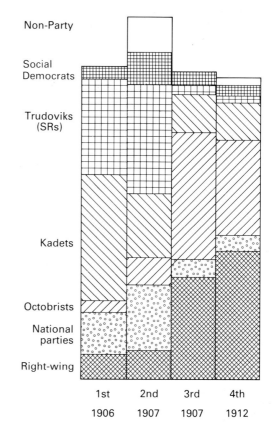

It seemed that the October Manifesto would never work. Some blamed the Duma members for their irresponsible behaviour and eagerness for sweeping change. Others thought that the Tsar was making no effort to co-operate, and would ignore any democratic assembly.

But these noisy arguments were carried on in public too; one big change since 1905 was the weakening of censorship. The police found it less easy to check free speech and to deal with outspoken politicians or newspapers. University students, free from interfering inspectors, enjoyed reading the new political newspapers with their forceful criticism of the Tsar. In 1912 even the Bolsheviks started their own paper in St Petersburg. Called *Pravda* ('Truth'), it soon sold 40,000 copies daily.

20

Stolypin

The Tsar found a new prime minister. Witte had been dismissed once more because he seemed arrogant and untrustworthy. In July 1906 Peter Arkadievich Stolypin took his place.

As governor of the province of Simbirsk, Stolypin had shown himself honest, energetic, tough and resourceful in facing rebels and restoring order. Nicholas brought him to St Petersburg to do the same for the whole Empire.

Stolypin was determined to make the Tsar's government work, if possible in harmony with the Duma. He secured a Duma that would co-operate by changing the rules for elections. All taxpayers voted, but now landowners and large property-owners were given more votes than peasants or workers. It made nonsense of democracy, but it did produce a Duma that worked.

The third Duma met in 1907, and sat for its full five years. The fourth Duma in 1912 was elected in the same way. In each there were small groups of left-wing extremists, perhaps twenty Social Democrats (both Mensheviks and Bolsheviks) and a dozen Trudoviks. There were rather more right-wing extremists, backing Tsarism against any change. The largest party were the Octobrists, conservative property-owners and industrialists, who worked with Stolypin though they sometimes criticised his actions. The Octobrists' leaders, an energetic businessman named Alexander Guchkov and a massive country gentleman, Michael Rodzianko, were successive presidents of the Duma. The Kadets, led by Miliukov, were also ready to support Stolypin until they could change the constitution to secure their own prime minister.

Revolutionaries denounced these Dumas as puppets that simply strengthened the Tsar's misrule. But others hoped that the Russian people at last were learning to make constitutional government work. Even the Tsar came to think that the Duma might have its uses. He told an Englishman in 1912, 'The Duma started too fast. Now it is slower, but better . . . and more lasting.'

Stolypin's first duty was to end revolutionary violence. He punished trouble-makers ruthlessly, putting to death over 2,000 in two years. He sought out and worked with businessmen, landowners and politicians ready to help in building a prosperous, stable country. But he knew that further changes were needed to prevent another disaster.

Peter Stolypin (1862–1911), the last strong minister of Tsarism, who hoped to avert revolution by allotting farms to the peasants.

Stolypin began many reforms. He increased the number of rural schools from about 100,000 to about 150,000. By 1914 they had seven million pupils; thirty years before there had been less than two million. Most Russian children now learned to read. Books and newspapers poured out for them.

Stolypin widened zemstvo membership and developed social insurance for workers. He legalised trade unions (but not strikes), reorganised the police, and helped ambitious young people to go east and settle in the developing lands of Siberia.

Above all, Stolypin hoped to build up a contented peasantry, seeking self-improvement rather than revolution. In 1906 he began a social revolution of his own, to give each peasant a farm saying, 'The small property owner is the cornerstone of any lasting political structure.' He ended the tight control of the mirs and the power of the Land Captains over village life and labour. If peasants farmed their own land, and could pass it on to their children or sell it, then Stolypin hoped they would be kept busy improving their holdings, and would support a strong government that allowed them to prosper in peace.

Stolypin wanted vast changes in a short time. In some villages peasants took over holdings at once, but elsewhere it was more complicated, as strips were scattered, or were exchanged each year. Similar changes had taken five centuries in Britain, causing much distress. But in Russia the splitting up of village fields and creation of new farms went ahead speedily; in ten years more than a quarter of peasants owned their own farms and many others were on the way to becoming independent. Generous government loans helped them improve their land with new methods and machinery. Ambitious farmers built up larger holdings and employed labourers. Some thought that such farmers set standards for the whole village to do better; others complained that such greedy *kulaks* ('fists', or tight-fisted farmers) upset traditional village co-operation. For every peasant pleased by the changes, others were annoyed by injustice, slowness or confusion.

Probably most Russians approved of the changes. The Octobrists backed Stolypin. The Kadets welcomed a move towards property-owning democracy. Mensheviks hoped that more capitalist farmers would mean more wage-earners ready to take over. Only SRs and Bolsheviks feared that Stolypin's reforms lessened their chance of a real rural revolution.

SR terrorists naturally tried to assassinate Stolypin. Many people admired his bravery when bombs wrecked his home and injured his children. Others were jealous, including some of the Tsar's closest friends and his police chiefs. In 1911 an SR shot and killed Stolypin; perhaps the assassin actually had help from the police. The Tsar never found another strong minister.

Towards revolution?

While Stolypin ruled, the possibility of revolution seemed to be receding. In the years after his death it looked closer. True, the farmers were doing very well following a run of good harvests. Trade was booming and industry growing fast. Soon, Russia could expect to be as prosperous as western countries. 'Give us ten more years and we are safe,' said an optimistic politician in 1914.

But booming business actually provoked discontent, as workers demanded better wages for themselves. On the remote goldfields along the River Lena in Siberia, workers went on strike for better living conditions in 1912. Troops fired at the mass of strikers, killing and wounding more than a hundred. Duma members were indignant, especially when the Tsar's minister complacently told them, 'So it has been always, so it will always be'. One lively young SR lawyer, Alexander Kerensky, was so outspoken in attacking the ministers that he became leader of the Trudoviks in the new Duma.

The Lena shooting seemed to arouse workers everywhere. In 1912 more than 700,000 went on strike. In the first half of 1914 alone, that number doubled. It seemed dangerously like 1905.

Spreading industrial unrest gave Social Democrat agents their chance. Most of the Party's leaders were far off in Austria or Switzerland, still arguing as Lenin clashed repeatedly with Mensheviks like Martov or Trotsky. Lenin's forcefulness and dedication attracted other exiles, who dreamed of revolution and a splendid socialist future. Most were in their twenties, intellectuals from wealthy families, and often Jewish. Many kept their real names secret, preferring nicknames. Lenin's closest follower was the voluble Zinoviev (real name, Radomylsky). His friend Kamenev (Rosenfeld) was a quiet, earnest writer, whom Lenin sent back to St Petersburg to run *Pravda*. Nicolai Bukharin was full of ideas, always theorising about the development of socialism. They argued, drank coffee and wrote lengthy political articles.

But Lenin knew the need to keep in touch with real workers inside Russia. He was a very active organiser, sending agents to contact underground groups, urging them to disrupt industry and hasten the bankruptcy of Tsarism. These Bolsheviks inside Russia were very different – ordinary people risking their jobs and freedom to prepare their fellow-workers for revolution. Lenin needed money from them to pay for agents and propaganda. Some raised it by theft and thuggery, methods which disgusted the Mensheviks, who feared that such crime would bring Marxism into disrepute.

Koba was still robbing banks for Party funds, and organising oil-workers in Georgia. He spoke and wrote vigorously against Mensheviks, and he belonged to one of the subject peoples whose support Lenin wanted. In 1912 Lenin summoned him to join the central committee of his Party, alongside the exiled intellectuals. Then he encouraged Koba

вар. виду		рост. 1 метр	сант.		Раса (если цвѣтнокожій)			
	Перенос. (глуб.)		Выс.врх.губ.		„Велич.“		Добн.-пос. ч.	
	Спинка Основ.		Выст.		„Особ.“		Нижн. ч. лиц.	
	Высота Выст. „Шир“		Бордюр.		Накл.		Выс. череп.	
			Толщин.		Высота		Особ.	
	Особ.		Особ.		Особ.			
	Верх. Низ.	Особ.						
	Прирост Поверхн.	Высота	Особ.					
Накл.	Проф. Выпич.	Разм. выст.	Особ.					
Нив. Верх.	Форм. уха Оттоп.		Таков.	ос.				

Stalin (1879–1953) as an underground revolutionary, from the files of the St Petersburg police, 1912–13.

to write, with some help from Bukharin, a booklet on *Marxism and the National Question*. It explained why good Georgians (and others) should support Bolshevism. In 1913 Koba returned to Russia, but he was soon arrested and sent to Siberia. He had taken to using another name: Stalin, 'Man of Steel'.

The Okhrana kept an eye on all Bolshevik activities. Some of Lenin's closest followers were secretly police agents. One trusted friend, who led the Bolsheviks in the Duma, actually arranged Stalin's arrest. But the police were worried. The disorders and strikes seemed to grow from too much free speech and Duma discussions, but attempts to tighten control only increased discontent. Trouble-makers sent to Siberia rarely found difficulty in escaping back to European Russia within months. Meanwhile, Kadets and Socialists in the Duma, especially Kerensky, constantly complained about police conduct.

They complained, too, about the ministers, and they did not trust the Tsar or his Empress, Alexandra. Stolypin's death had

Rasputin as a cartoonist saw him, with Nicholas and Alexandra as puppets.

ended co-operation. Nicholas seemed incapable of finding effective ministers, or of supporting those he appointed. He listened not to the Duma's advice but to his wife, friends and favourites. One friend was particularly disliked: the unsavoury Rasputin.

Rasputin, 'Immoral One', was what most people called Gregory Efimovich, a peasant holy man from Siberia. He was a wanderer whose uncouth appearance and outrageous behaviour upset St Petersburg society. Claiming mysterious powers, he convinced the Empress that he alone could cure the painful and dangerous haemophilia of her young son Alexis, heir to the imperial throne. Perhaps through hypnotism, Rasputin relieved Alexis' pain and stopped the bleeding. Alexandra, desperately grateful, believed that Gregory was

sent from God; her husband, she insisted, should follow the holy man's advice.

Nicholas had his own reasons for heeding Rasputin. This Siberian was only too obviously a peasant, very different from the clean, clever, westernised politicians in the narrow world of St Petersburg. He spoke for the people of the villages throughout the Empire.

In fact Rasputin's advice was sometimes shrewd. In 1914 he warned the Tsar against going to war, for war had nearly destroyed Tsarism in 1905. Now he said, 'With war will come the end of Russia and yourselves.' On this occasion, though, Nicholas heeded not the peasant holy man but the ministers, politicians and newspapers.

The First World War, 1914–18

The war, when it came, was popular with all sections of the population. Russia had been humiliated too often. Japan had beaten her in 1905 while Europe sneered. In 1908 Austria-Hungary had seized the provinces of Bosnia and Herzegovina from under the nose of Russia's friend and ally, Serbia. Russia had threatened, but had been too weak to help fellow Slavs. Now, in 1914, Serbia once more needed help against Austria. Despite the fact that Germany stood beside Austria, the Tsar and his people were determined to give that help. Moreover, they could count on powerful allies – Britain and France.

Russians everywhere rallied behind the Tsar. 'Our first duty is to preserve our country, one and undivided,' said Paul Miliukov, to wild applause from the Duma. 'Let us lay aside our domestic differences.' Tsar, Duma and people were united to face the enemy, and it was natural to change their capital's German-sounding name to the Russian Petrograd. The armies gathered and millions of ordinary Russians filled the ranks to serve their Tsar.

Most Social Democrats, even, rallied to support the government, dismaying those like Trotsky who hoped that workers throughout Europe would unite to overthrow their rulers and prevent war. Lenin, in exile in Austrian Poland, was furious, for this surge of loyalty might end any hope of revolution. The Austrians arrested him as a spy, but released him to return to Switzerland as soon as they found that he was no friend to Tsarist Russia.

As at the start of any war there were terrible muddles, and

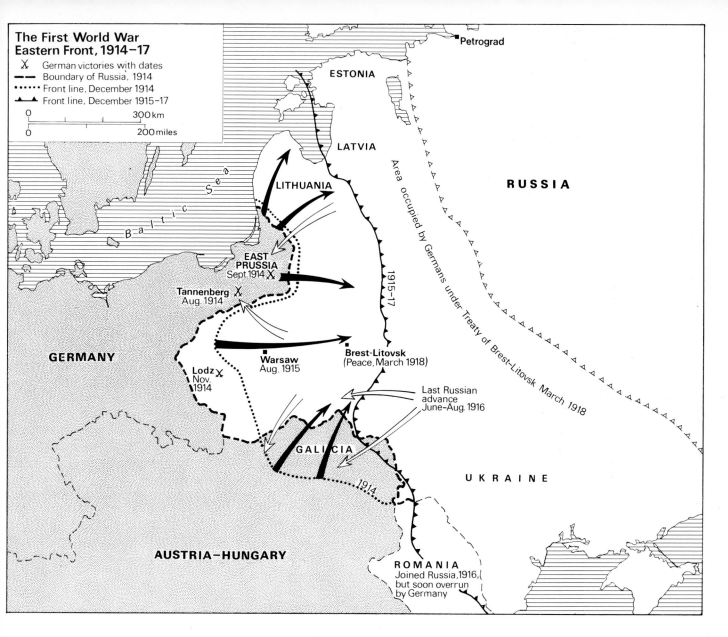

The First World War
Eastern Front, 1914–17

X   German victories with dates
– – – Boundary of Russia, 1914
••••• Front line, December 1914
▲▲▲ Front line, December 1915–17

0   300 km
0   200 miles

Petrograd

ESTONIA

LATVIA

LITHUANIA

RUSSIA

Area occupied by Germans under Treaty of Brest-Litovsk March 1918

EAST
PRUSSIA
Sept.1914 X

1915–17

Tannenberg X
Aug. 1914

GERMANY

Brest-Litovsk
(Peace, March 1918)

Warsaw
Aug. 1915

Lodz X
Nov.
1914

Last Russian
advance
June–Aug. 1916

GALICIA

UKRAINE

1914

AUSTRIA–HUNGARY

ROMANIA
Joined Russia,1916,
but soon overrun
by Germany

for Russia they led to early disaster. Two armies advancing into Germany were destroyed through a combination of confusion, bad generalship and ill luck. Against Austria the Russians were at first more successful. For two hideous years slaughter continued along the vast Front, with German armies pressing deep into western Russia. Sometimes the Russians scored remarkable successes; in 1916 General Brusilov shattered Austria's armies, and the Germans had to rescue their

25

allies. More often the Russians had to retreat, with immense losses of men and weapons. Lice, dirt, frost, mud, starvation, shortages and lack of medical care made conditions terrible. By the end of 1916 more than a million Russians had been killed, three million captured and four million wounded. Yet the armies had grown steadily as more and more peasants were called up and, despite the losses, fourteen million men were still under arms, determined to crush Germany.

By late 1916, too, lack of weapons had largely been overcome. In 1915 Russian industrialists formed War Industry Committees to organise arms production, and the output of guns and shells grew rapidly. Russian heavy industry went through a little revolution of its own to meet wartime demand. But bottlenecks, wastage, muddle and an over-worked railway system often meant that weapons failed to arrive when and where they were needed. Meanwhile, many businesses made huge profits, though their workers found wages hardly kept up with fast-rising prices.

Russian soldiers fought doggedly, though sometimes despairing men deserted, or shot off a finger to avoid further service. New recruits were herded into the cities, ill-disciplined and apprehensive, waiting to be sent to the slaughter. Since most junior officers from gentry or loyal peasant families had been killed off early in the fighting, their commanders were now often educated young men from the middle classes, anxious to see the war ended speedily and efficiently.

The Tsar saw it as his duty to direct the war himself. Others had different ideas and were anxious to play their part; the generals, the Duma, the War Industry Committees and the zemstvos all offered advice. The Tsar usually thanked and ignored them. The result was that whenever things went wrong at the Front, in arms production, or in food supplies for the cities packed with refugees and recruits, the Tsar was blamed. In 1915 Nicholas went to military headquarters to take command. That left the Empress in charge of Petrograd, and she distrusted the Duma politicians, suspecting that they wanted to upset Tsarist rule while the Tsar was busy with the war. Equally, the politicians distrusted Alexandra and her friend Rasputin. But when they protested and pleaded, the Tsar simply dismissed the Duma and appointed ministers approved by Rasputin.

Military disasters, industrial muddles, profiteering and inflation, constant food shortages in the cities, distrust of the Empress and her favourite, all led to growing discontent. At last, in December 1916, a group of the Tsar's relatives and supporters decided that desperate action was needed. Luring Rasputin to one of their houses, they poisoned, shot, battered and drowned him in a messy effort to rescue Nicholas from his influence.

The February Revolution

Rasputin's murder came too late to save the Tsar. Already other politicians and generals were planning to remove Nicholas as soon as there was an opportunity. Early in March (late February by the old calendar) events in Petrograd gave them a chance. Snow and ice held up food supplies, and long queues formed at the bakeries. At the same time many factory workers, seeking a 50 per cent pay rise, came out on strike or were locked out by their bosses. Anxious and angry crowds roamed the city's slushy streets. Some began demanding a new government. Perhaps secret German money encouraged them; perhaps the police and ministers deliberately allowed unrest to come into the open so as to crush it more effectively; but it seems that most demonstrations were unplanned and unexpected.

This time the soldiers did not behave as they had in 1905. At first they dispersed the crowds, but then some refused to fire, and even helped demonstrators against the police. Some turned against their officers and joined the crowds, calling for the overthrow of Tsar and government. Without reliable troops the ministers were helpless.

The Duma leaders seized their opportunity. On 12 March (or 27 February) they met in the Tauride Palace, which was surrounded by excited workers and soldiers, calling for action and chanting the *Marseillaise*, the song of revolution. The politicians hurriedly formed into a committee to take charge and restore order.

But the Duma committee had a rival. On that same day factory workers all over Petrograd voted by show of hands to elect a soviet, as they had in 1905. The workers' soviet met that evening, also in the Tauride Palace. Some twenty soldiers from mutinous regiments joined it, making the first "Soviet of Workers' and Soldiers' Deputies". It too chose an Executive Committee (ExCom for short) to look after the interests of its supporters.

Alexander Kerensky (1881–1970), the Trudovik lawyer who, in the Provisional Government of 1917, was minister for Justice, then for War, and finally Prime Minister, visiting troops at the front in the hope of encouraging them against the Germans.

The February Revolution was over in less than a week, with perhaps 1,200 police, soldiers and workers killed or injured. Once Petrograd had revolted, the rest of Russia followed. Tsar Nicholas set off from army headquarters to restore order, but his train was stopped by striking railway workers. Cut off from his army and his capital, he could do nothing. The Duma committee demanded his abdication, and Nicholas obediently signed it, hoping thus to re-unite Russia against the German enemy. The Duma committee became the 'Provisional Government' until elections could be held and a new constitution could be prepared. But the Provisional Government had to heed the demands of the Soviet ExCom, which spoke for the workers and soldiers.

The Duma leaders were eager to rule. They had long criticised mis-management and tyranny; this was their chance to do better. One man in particular seemed to know what had to be done: Alexander Kerensky, youthful, wiry, constantly on the move and pausing only to deliver brief, rousing speeches to anyone listening, had found his chance to build a free Russia. The other members of the government were older, steadier politicians. Prince George Lvov, a distinguished Liberal who had long chaired outspoken zemstvo committees, became Prime Minister. Miliukov, of the Kadets, seemed strongest and steadiest of all, as Foreign Minister. The Octobrist Guchkov became War Minister and Kerensky Minister for Justice.

Kerensky, popular with the workers, had also been elected to the ExCom, so he linked the two bodies in their different rooms at the Tauride. The Soviet was a chaotic group, changing from day to day, and listening to anyone with ideas or complaints. Its Menshevik and SR leaders generally left the middle-class liberals of the Provisional Government to run the country and fight the war. In time, they believed, the socialists would take over; but for the moment they were mainly interested in protecting workers and soldiers from harsh employers and bullying officers. So the Provisional Government and Petrograd Soviet each went its own way.

Millions of Russians felt suddenly and miraculously free from age-old oppression. Now, they thought, they could talk and write freely, eat more, get rid of rent-collectors, tax-gatherers and profiteers, and finish the war triumphantly. The old Russia of the Tsars had gone for ever.

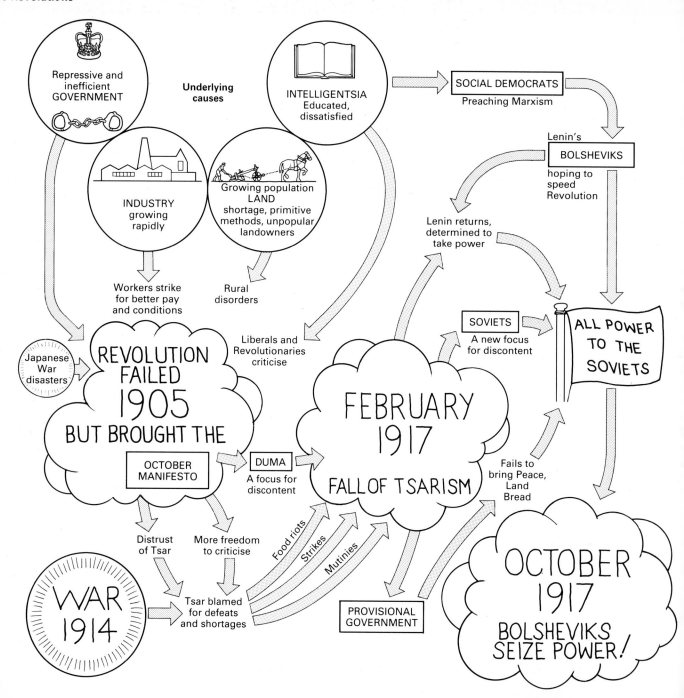

Repressive and inefficient GOVERNMENT

Underlying causes

INTELLIGENTSIA Educated, dissatisfied

SOCIAL DEMOCRATS

Preaching Marxism

Lenin's

BOLSHEVIKS

hoping to speed Revolution

INDUSTRY growing rapidly

Growing population LAND shortage, primitive methods, unpopular landowners

Lenin returns, determined to take power

Workers strike for better pay and conditions

Rural disorders

Liberals and Revolutionaries criticise

SOVIETS

A new focus for discontent

ALL POWER TO THE SOVIETS

Japanese War disasters

REVOLUTION FAILED 1905 BUT BROUGHT THE

FEBRUARY 1917 FALL OF TSARISM

Fails to bring Peace, Land Bread

OCTOBER MANIFESTO

DUMA

A focus for discontent

Distrust of Tsar

More freedom to criticise

Food riots

Strikes

Mutinies

WAR 1914

Tsar blamed for defeats and shortages

PROVISIONAL GOVERNMENT

OCTOBER 1917 BOLSHEVIKS SEIZE POWER!

3 November 1917: the Bolsheviks seize power

Lenin's return

In Switzerland, as Lenin wondered gloomily whether his generation would ever see the revolution he dreamed of, a fellow exile burst in with news of a rising in Petrograd.

If the Tsar's government was collapsing, Lenin wanted to be on the spot. He heard that his supporters, Kamenev and Stalin, were already back in Petrograd from Siberian exile, and were using *Pravda* to rally all socialists behind Russia's new, free government. Tsarism had been toppled. The time would come to overthrow the capitalist regime that had replaced it, but first the newly-freed people must unite to protect their country from the Germans.

That was not Lenin's view; he thought revolution should come first. But it would be weeks before he could reach Petrograd. The German authorities agreed to help him get home, trusting him to wreck Russia's war effort. In a train sealed from all contact with the German people, Lenin and his friends journeyed to neutral Sweden and on to Finland. Lenin's train finally steamed into Petrograd's Finland Station late on 16 April. *Pravda* told everyone that the most famous of exiles and wisest of socialists was coming home. A noisy mob of soldiers, sailors and workers turned out to meet him. A Menshevik eye-witness, Nicolai Sukhanov, wrote afterwards:

> The train was very late. But at long last it arrived. A thunderous *Marseillaise* boomed forth along the platform, and shouts of welcome rang out . . . Lenin . . . wore a round cap, his face looked frozen, and there was a magnificent bouquet in his hands . . . Chkheidze [Menshevik chairman of the Soviet] pronounced the 'speech of welcome'.
> 'Comrade Lenin, in the name of the Petrograd Soviet and of the whole Revolution we welcome you to Russia . . . *But* – we think the principal task of revolutionary democracy is now defence of the Revolution . . . We hope you will pursue these goals together with us.'
> Lenin plainly knew just how to behave . . . Turning away

from the ExCom delegation altogether, he made this reply:
> 'Dear Comrades, soldiers, sailors and workers! I am happy to greet in you the victorious Russian Revolution, and greet you as vanguard of the world proletarian army . . . The world-wide Socialist Revolution has dawned . . . The Russian Revolution has prepared the way and opened a new epoch. Long live the world-wide Socialist Revolution!'

Under glaring electric lights outside the station, Lenin climbed on a car bonnet to speak to the crowd. He demanded an end to 'shameful imperialist slaughter' and 'the lies and frauds of capitalism'. Then the whole crowd, band playing and red banners waving, marched off with their new leader to the Bolshevik headquarters.

Lenin was demanding a new kind of revolution. He knew exactly what changes he wanted, and he cared little for what was actually happening in Russia, for middle-class ministers or muddled Mensheviks. Other socialists might wait for Russia to fit Marxist theories, for industrial workers to gain strength and overthrow capitalism. But Lenin was ready to re-shape Marxism and Russia to fit each other, to use Russia's peasant masses to back revolution. From the moment of his arrival, he and his followers set about destroying the Provisional Government.

The Provisional Government

Prince Lvov's government despised these revolutionaries believing that they attracted only irresponsible and unpatriotic hot-heads. The ministers were anxious to finish the war first, and then get on with building a westernised, democratic Russia. Within days of taking over, they freed political prisoners, abolished the death penalty, ordered an eight-hour working day, scrapped controls over trade unions, newspapers, public meetings and religious worship. As Lenin said, even in the midst of a terrible war they made Russia the most free country in the world. In *Dr Zhivago*, Boris Pasternak remembered it as 'real freedom, freedom dropped from the sky, freedom beyond our expectations'. The Provisional Government had splendid plans. They wanted all Russians to elect a Constituent Assembly to plan a new form of government. They intended to share out the great estates among poor peasants. They hoped for a swift ending to the war now that they had ended Tsarist bungling.

But all over Russia, peasants and workers were already acting for themselves. They wanted solid improvements *now*, and could see no reason to wait for a new constitution. They knew that Tsarist rule, with its officials, taxes and regulations, was over, but they were suspicious of any government that attempted to interfere.

Trouble exploded when Miliukov, as Foreign Minister, promised Russia's continued help to Britain and France against Germany. Every Russian wanted to win the war, but the Petrograd crowds milling round the ExCom meetings cared nothing for the Tsar's allies. They heard socialists arguing that if only other nations would overthrow their leaders as the Russians had, then workers everywhere could stop the bloodshed. Miliukov was committing Russia to fight the Tsar's war for power and territory, and they called angrily for his resignation. Prince Lvov gave way, and in May Miliukov went. The leaders of the Soviet themselves, Mensheviks and SRs, were brought in to strengthen the government. Kerensky, most prominent of the SRs, was promoted to War Minister, and went off to the front to rouse the armies to action.

The Germans were watching and waiting. There had been no serious fighting for months, and many Russians had taken the opportunity to desert, heading home to find out how their villages had fared in the upheavals. Now Kerensky called on them to fight again, not for Russia's allies but for their newly-freed country. Early in July the Russian armies attacked. For a few days they advanced, but many soldiers were half-hearted. When they met resistance and found victory no easier than under Tsarism, they turned against the officers urging them on, or quietly went home. The Germans counter-attacked and advanced deeper into Russia.

The July Days

Kerensky dashed back to Petrograd to find new troubles. Restive crowds were once more clamouring on the streets. They had freedom, but no food. Although crops were good, the overloaded railways could not bring enough. Prices were soaring ever higher, as the government printed money to meet expenses instead of collecting taxes. Bad news from the Front provoked street demonstrations, and again soldiers from the garrison and sailors from the island base of Kronstadt joined them. They seized important buildings, and there was some shooting. For two or three days, the 'July Days', Petrograd was as turbulent as it had been in February.

This time there was no revolution. The rioters found no leaders. The Soviet, supporting the Provisional Government, did not want fresh disorders. Lenin was not sure whether the discontented could overthrow the Government while it still had the Soviet behind it. Some Bolsheviks did urge on the crowds; so did Leon Trotsky, just returned from exile in the United States and impatient as ever for action.

The Government was in a stronger position than the Tsar's ministers had been. Fresh troops were brought in. The sailors were persuaded to go back to Kronstadt. Word was spread that Bolshevik trouble-makers were behind the disorders, and the ministers published details of the money Lenin had received from the Germans. The mob's anger turned sharply against the Bolsheviks. *Pravda*'s presses were wrecked, Lenin hid in disguise, and other leaders were arrested. Trotsky, who had joined with the Bolsheviks, angrily demanded to be arrested too.

Kerensky in charge

The Provisional Government had won, but felt badly shaken by the July Days. A new leader was needed, and the vigorous Kerensky seemed the man for the job. He replaced Lvov as Prime Minister, heading a team of keen reformers. They planned elections for the Constituent Assembly to take place in November, and meanwhile Kerensky promised to be firm with trouble-makers; too much freedom was not working.

Kerensky found he could not check the growing anarchy. In the countryside, villagers seized and split up the landowners' great estates. The young mechanic, Nikita Khrushchev, hurried to his old home to make sure his family got their share.

4 July 1917: a crowd on Nevsky Prospekt in Petrograd, dispersed by troops supporting the Provisional Government.

In towns, factories and army barracks there were strikes and mutinies. Workers feared that employers might sack them, cut wages, or close down altogether. In disorderly mass-meetings they elected their noisiest comrades (like Khrushchev) to their own soviets, and appointed the toughest as 'Red Guards' to protect them from the bosses. Usually local Bolsheviks took the lead, spreading the Party's ideas and enthusiasm.

Faced with the rising lawlessness and violence, many Russians looked for a strong leader to restore order. Kerensky's commander-in-chief, General Kornilov, seemed an obvious person. He was from a humble background, brave, and not very clever; he had led his troops successfully and managed to keep some discipline. Now crowds cheered him, expecting him to pull Russia together by the same forceful methods. Even Kerensky hoped that Kornilov might help him suppress trouble-makers and establish stable government.

But when, in September, Kornilov started moving his armies towards Petrograd and called on all Russians to aid him in 'saving our native land', Kerensky realised the danger: he might be overthrown if Kornilov made himself dictator.

So Kerensky called desperately for help to 'save the Revolution'. He appealed to the soldiers and sailors in Petrograd, to the factory workers and Red Guards, to the Soviet, and even to his enemies the Bolsheviks. He had rifles handed out to anyone who would help defend the city. Kornilov found his troop trains stopped by torn-up railway lines, heard of resistance being planned, and faced mutiny among his own followers. He gave up.

Kerensky's government survived, but disorder continued, and again people looked elsewhere for a firm hand to save Russia. The leaders of the Petrograd Soviet, and of other workers', peasants' and soldiers' soviets everywhere, denounced Kerensky as weak and woolly, all bluster and no action. Some soviets talked of taking power into their own hands. The Bolsheviks encouraged such ideas. They claimed that they had led the workers in saving Russia from Kornilov. Now they had weapons in their hands, they controlled the Red Guards, and they dominated more and more soviets. Lenin saw his opportunity. 'All Power to the Soviets!' he demanded, and the slogan was taken up by workers and soldiers everywhere.

In October the fiery Trotsky, newly freed from prison and

now whole-heartedly behind Lenin, was elected chairman of the Petrograd Soviet. An 'All-Russian Congress of Soviets' was arranged for 7 November, to bring together representatives from the whole country. That Congress, urged on by Bolsheviks, would be certain to challenge Kerensky.

The Provisional Government, once so optimistic and so popular, seemed on the brink of failure. Kerensky's inspiring language was leading nowhere. He had neither Kornilov's army nor, as yet, a Constituent Assembly to back his rule, and he faced an impossible situation. Until he could finish the war he could neither satisfy popular impatience for land and democracy nor check ruthless enemies from undermining his efforts. Those enemies now prepared for his overthrow, using the soviets and the mob, which had destroyed one feeble government in March and was ready to turn on its successor.

The October Revolution

October in Petrograd was miserable. Queues for milk, bread, sugar and tobacco waited in chill rain under grey skies. Mud was everywhere, slippery and clinging. Street-lights were few and far between in the lengthening evenings.

Lenin, still in hiding, saw discontent building up once more. The moment had come. All over Russia Bolsheviks led the local soviets, and many SRs backed their demands for change. The All-Russian Congress of Soviets was due to meet soon, and he expected its Bolshevik members to jockey it into taking over 'All Power' from the Provisional Government. The Party must be ready to back Congress with force, and the Bolshevik leaders turned themselves into a 'policy committee' of seven to direct the takeover. This *Politburo* included Lenin, Trotsky, Zinoviev, Kamenev and Stalin.

Lenin demanded prompt action. Others urged caution. Zinoviev and Kamenev knew that the majority of workers did not yet support the Bolsheviks. They also feared another disaster like the July Days, and even published their objections in the press. Lenin promptly printed his own furious answer: the time to act decisively was *now*.

While Lenin argued, cajoled and threatened, Trotsky planned. As chairman of the Soviet, he led a small 'Military Revolutionary Committee'. Through it he made sure that everyone who supported the Bolsheviks knew just what to do. He prepared orders to troops and sailors to seize Petrograd's

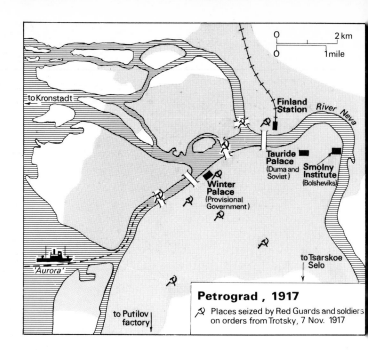

Petrograd, 1917

Places seized by Red Guards and soldiers on orders from Trotsky, 7 Nov. 1917

strong points, arms factories and railway stations on behalf of the Soviet. He appeared everywhere to make violent speeches, warning of danger from Kerensky, demanding help to win 'victory for the Revolution that will give land, bread and peace'.

On 7 November (25 October by the old calendar) most of Petrograd's people worked or queued as usual. But at the Smolny Institute, once a fashionable girls' school, there had been bustle and activity all night. The Smolny was headquarters for both the Bolsheviks and the Military Committee, and Trotsky was issuing streams of orders. Sometimes contradictory orders came from the government, but most soldiers chose to obey the Soviet. They and the Red Guards moved off before dawn to seize their objectives. The crew of the cruiser *Aurora* forced their commander to bring his ship up the River Neva into the heart of the city, and in the glare of its searchlights sailors helped pro-Soviet troops take control of the bridges. At 10 a.m. Trotsky announced confidently that the Provisional Government had fallen, though the ministers were still busy in the Winter Palace, and Kerensky had gone to find loyal troops. Late in the afternoon Soviet forces closed in on the Palace. At 9 p.m. the *Aurora* opened fire, and the Palace's defenders realised they faced a losing battle. Red Guards forced their way in, and there were scuffles in the corridors. There was little bloodshed, but soon after midnight the Winter Palace and the ministers were captured.

A few hours earlier, late in the evening, the Congress of Soviets had met. Trotsky told them that Soviet troops controlled capital and country. Mensheviks, SRs, every member who stood for law and democracy, protested vehemently. This, they shouted, was illegal and violent. It would bring bitter divisions and civil war. The hall seethed as some speakers acclaimed the new leaders and others passionately denounced them. Finally Martov, Lenin's old friend, led the Mensheviks and many SRs out. They would have nothing to do with the Bolshevik coup. Trotsky sneered after them, 'You have played your role. Go where you belong: to the rubbish-heap of history.'

Next day what was left of the Congress approved a new government for Russia. Fifteen leading Bolsheviks became *commissars* (as the revolutionaries called their ministers and officials) and Lenin headed the new Council of People's Commissars, or *Sovnarkom*.

Lenin and Communist rule

The Sovnarkom acted swiftly. Bolsheviks already controlled Petrograd, and soon took over many other towns, though there were five days of fighting before Moscow fell. They had no time to lose. Their many enemies were disorganised for the moment, but soon they would strike back. If the new rulers could put their Marxist ideas into practice, could show what a workers' state really meant, then all good Russians would rally to them, and so would the oppressed workers of the world. They must build socialism speedily from the ruins of capitalism.

'Land, bread and peace!', the Bolsheviks had promised. On their very first day they issued decrees:

> The workers' and peasants' government . . . calls upon the belligerent peoples and their governments to start immediate negotiations for a just, democratic peace.
>
> Landlord ownership of land is abolished forthwith.

Providing bread was not so simple. The best the commissars could do for the moment was to order arrest and punishment for profiteers, as enemies of the people.

There were many other decrees:

Newspapers criticising the new government were closed as 'counter-revolutionary'.

Army ranks and titles were abolished; soldiers were to elect their officers.

The Church lost its property and privileges.

All nationalities of the Empire were free and equal, with the right to self-government.

The State took over banks, factories and transport.

Members of the Congress of Soviets were sent home as soon as they had approved the first decrees. There need be no more argument in the palaces of Petrograd. When the long-awaited Constituent Assembly met in January, with a large SR majority, it was promptly closed. It was out of date, said Lenin, a mere talking-shop for the Revolution's enemies. There could be no going back, and the Bolsheviks alone could speak for the workers.

For Bolsheviks the Revolution was sacred. It marked the rebirth of Russia and set an example to all nations. Soon they dropped their Russian name to become the Communist Party, proclaiming their ideals to the world. Anyone questioning their achievement or purpose was 'misguided' and perhaps dangerous. From now on there could be but one political party in Russia. Mensheviks and SRs were tolerated for a while, but then their parties too were abolished.

The Communists had won power on behalf of the workers, the 'proletariat'. Until the workers learned to use their new power correctly and live as good Communists, it was the Party's duty to lead and educate. Nothing must obstruct this work. In December 1917 a Sovnarkom decree set up an 'Extraordinary Commission' (*Cheka* in its shortened Russian form) to fight counter-revolution. It was, 'To persecute and break up all acts of counter-revolution . . . To watch the press, saboteurs, strikers and the Socialist-Revolutionaries.'

The Cheka was rather like the Tsar's Okhrana (abolished by the Provisional Government). It soon became an essential instrument of Communist rule. It changed its name several times over the next three decades, and since 1953 has been known as the Committee for State Security, the KGB.

There were only 300,000 Party members among 140,000,000

Lenin addressing workers outside the Putilov (later renamed Kirov) Works in Petrograd. The Soviet artist Brodsky painted many pictures glorifying the Revolution and its leaders. He contrasts the dynamic, inspiring Lenin with the mass of thoughtful, appreciative listeners.

Russians, but those 300,000 believed absolutely in the Party and leader. Because Lenin had created the Party, defined its policy and directed its rise, he was its undisputed head. He had argumentative colleagues, and sometimes only got his way after furious disputes, but in the end his burning determination proved irresistible.

Lenin and the Party's Politburo were the real rulers of Russia, while the Sovnarkom (all Communists, and mostly Politburo members) was the nominal government. Politburo and Sovnarkom gave the orders; the Party Congress and Congress of Soviets approved them. The two congresses consisted of dedicated Communists or sympathisers, elected by loyal Party members or dutiful citizens. They heard their leaders explain, then discussed and argued; only rarely was there serious disagreement.

Though the Communists tightened control inside Russia, beyond it they had little success. Foreign workers could not or would not help as Lenin had hoped. The German workers in Germany's armies obeyed their commanders and pressed on with the invasion of Russia. Soon, it seemed, Germany might overthrow the Communists and set up its own puppet government. As the price of peace Germany made huge demands – independence from Russia for Poland, Finland, the Baltic provinces, and the Ukraine. These would become German satellites.

The Communist leaders were divided. 'Neither war nor peace,' said Trotsky; refuse to fight, but do not accept these terms. The Germans pushed on with their advance. Fight back, urged Bukharin, unleash a revolutionary crusade against Germany, even if we perish in the attempt. But Lenin knew that unless they made peace, even on Germany's terms, Communist rule could be destroyed. He argued his colleagues into acceptance, and in March 1918 they made peace at Brest-Litovsk. Russia's Empire was in ruins, and more than a third of the population and agricultural land was lost. But the Party still controlled what was left. Lenin had preserved his base for world revolution.

World revolution still seemed far off, and Lenin moved his capital from the dangerously exposed Petrograd (with its troublesome crowds) back to Moscow, in the heart of old Russia. Communist parties did form in many other countries, and in 1919 Lenin set up the *Comintern* (Communist International) to draw them under Russian leadership. But nowhere else did Communists manage to take *and* hold power. Until workers elsewhere were stronger and better organised, it seemed all the more necessary to secure the workers' base in Russia.

Civil War, 1918–20

During the summer after their seizure of power the Communist leaders found enemies gathering all round: land-owners, industrialists, army officers, Christians resenting attacks on the Church, and all who had lost power or property. Opposition from such people was to be expected.

What was more worrying was that many soldiers, peasants and workers were coming to think that Communism did no more for them than earlier governments; and, having learned to argue and defy their old masters, they were ready to treat the commissars the same way. Villagers, fearing the Communist State would take their lands, turned to their old SR friends. Sometimes Communist officials were attacked and even lynched. Some local leaders, facing continued disorder, set up small, popular republics of their own, which collapsed

Trotsky with Red Army men; a propaganda photograph stressing his leadership.

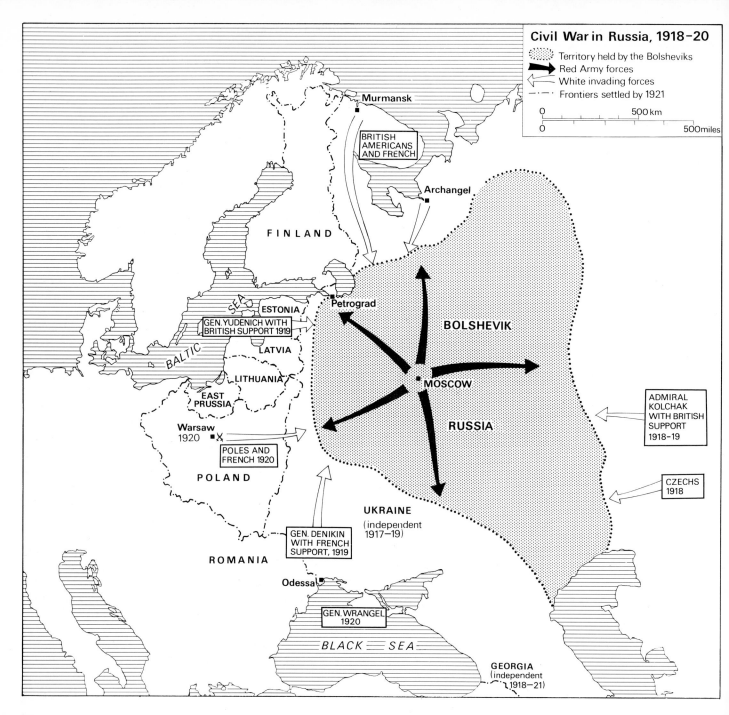

Civil War in Russia, 1918–20

- Territory held by the Bolsheviks
- Red Army forces
- White invading forces
- Frontiers settled by 1921

0   500 km
0   500 miles

Murmansk

BRITISH AMERICANS AND FRENCH

Archangel

FINLAND

BOLSHEVIK

Petrograd

ESTONIA

GEN. YUDENICH WITH BRITISH SUPPORT 1919

BALTIC SEA

LATVIA

LITHUANIA

MOSCOW

EAST PRUSSIA

RUSSIA

ADMIRAL KOLCHAK WITH BRITISH SUPPORT 1918–19

Warsaw 1920

POLES AND FRENCH 1920

CZECHS 1918

POLAND

GEN. DENIKIN WITH FRENCH SUPPORT, 1919

UKRAINE (independent 1917–19)

ROMANIA

Odessa

GEN. WRANGEL 1920

BLACK SEA

GEORGIA (independent 1918–21)

in a few weeks. Armed bands wandered in search of food. Most Russians just hoped for firm government, peace and prosperity; but some prepared to fight to get rid of the new rulers.

Many SRs, knowing how easily they would triumph if only there were free elections, and infuriated by the Communists' refusal to share power, began to think of their old tactics: assassination. In July 1918 two SRs killed the new German ambassador. In August another assassinated the head of the Petrograd Cheka, and on the same day a woman badly wounded Lenin himself.

The rulers struck back ferociously. The Cheka lumped all enemies together: 'counter-revolutionaries, spies, speculators, hooligans, saboteurs and other parasites' would all be 'mercilessly shot by the Commission's detachments on the spot'. There were no trials. Hostages were shot in thousands all over Russia. Often people were killed simply because they were former members of the wealthier classes. The ex-Tsar and his family were wiped out to make sure that the peasants would have no 'Little Father' to turn to. This ruthless slaughter of possible enemies was far worse than anything seen in the days of Tsarism.

The 'Red Terror' frightened many into submission, others into resistance. 'White' armies gathered as Russians were forced to take sides for or against Communism. Each side tried to terrorise the other by killing its supporters. The Communists held on to the heartland around Moscow, but from each direction former Tsarist generals led ramshackle armies against it. The Whites had overall superiority in numbers, but they never succeeded in working together. Vast distances and different aims separated them. Some wanted a new Tsar, others a military dictator, a liberal democracy, a socialist republic, an independent Ukraine, and so on. They had half-hearted help from Germans, Poles, Czechs, French, British, Americans and Japanese at different times and places, who feared the spread of Communist ideas. But these foreign intruders aroused resentment and suspicion, and in the end they deserted their White allies and went home.

In contrast Lenin's followers were united and single-minded, committed to their cause and fighting for survival. Trotsky was the hero of the Civil War. He built a new Red Army, recruiting thousands of former Tsarist officers to train and lead it. They knew their families would suffer if they failed him. He placed reliable Communists as 'political commissars' and joint commanders in each unit, making it clear that if troops weakened in battle the commissars would be shot first and the officers next. He himself dashed from one battle-front to another in his armoured train, issuing orders to stand firm and to shoot suspected traitors, cowards or muddlers. Trotsky's methods were crude, but they worked. Nikita Khrushchev was among the thousands who were drawn into the Red Army and turned into tough, enthusiastic and efficient soldiers. Their drive and ruthlessness triumphed over one White army after another. By 1920 all of European Russia and the Ukraine were back under Moscow's control. Only the Poles were able to defeat the Red Army, and the Communists decided it was wiser to let Poland, Finland and the Baltic states go their separate ways.

Change of course: from War Communism to NEP

Two years of Civil War brought more hardship than ever. Communism of a kind, 'War Communism', was established in an effort to produce the food and supplies the government needed. All had to 'give according to their abilities'. Detachments of workers with machine guns went into villages to make sure that the peasants did so. Factory workers were compelled to stay at their jobs for long hours. All should have received 'according to their needs', and the government tried to provide food for workers and their families. But the system simply did not work. Peasants refused to produce food that would be taken from them. In the cities much was sold on the black market, and shooting the black marketeers just added to the shortages. Money lost all value, and people bartered for anything available. Factories stopped through lack of power, light, materials and workers.

By the start of 1921 the Whites had been defeated, but economic disaster loomed. Food production was below two-thirds of pre-war level, industrial output below one-third. Famine and epidemics spread everywhere. More people died from hunger and disease than from the Red and White Terrors.

In March 1921 it seemed that the events of March 1917 might be repeated. Food was shorter than ever in Petrograd; there were strikes and angry public meetings, despite the Cheka. Discontent spread, as it had before, to the island naval

Famine, October 1921. Starving children in a camp near the Volga.

economic miracle. Two changes of Party policy were announced.

First, economic relaxation: a New Economic Policy (NEP). Socialism would take one step back in order to move two steps forward later. Much capitalist freedom would be restored. Grain seizures would end, and the peasants might grow and sell as they pleased so long as each handed over a quota to the State. Trade controls were lifted, and many factories were handed over to private owners. But the 'Commanding Heights of the Economy', the great industrial plants, remained in State hands; and the State remained in Party hands.

Second, a tighter political grip: the Party Congress agreed to a motion 'On the Unity of the Party'. There were to be no more divisions or arguments within the Communist Party. 'We don't need an opposition, Comrades,' said Lenin. Communists must stand together, with no internal cliques, factions or pressure groups. Anyone disagreeing with the Party line would be expelled.

The period of revolution had ended. It had produced something very different from what Lenin and his followers had intended. The Party was as firmly in control as the Tsar had once been, and its methods were similar to the Tsar's, though more ruthless. But it had not won people over to Communism, either in Russia or outside, so it dared not allow the freedom it had hoped for, nor set up the socialist society it believed in.

Lenin was paralysed by a stroke in 1922, and died early in 1924. His colleagues staged elaborate ceremonies of grief and mourning. They placed his preserved body on display in a splendid mausoleum beside the Kremlin in Red Square, where it became the object of pilgrimage. They lavished praise on Lenin's memory, his words and deeds. Henceforth the cult of wise, all-seeing Lenin was to replace the Bible for good Communists.

base of Kronstadt, 26 kilometres (16 miles) away in the Gulf of Finland. In 1917 Trotsky had called the mutinous sailors 'the pride and glory of the Revolution'. Now, the sailors complained that 'The power of the police monarchy has fallen into the hands of the Communists, who instead of freedom offer the workers constant fear from the torture-chambers of the Cheka.' They complained that Communists had more bureaucratic officials than the Tsar. They wanted free speech, a free press, free trade unions, free sale of peasant grain, free workers' political parties, and free elections for the soviets.

The Kronstadt Rebellion frightened the Communist leaders as nothing else had. Trotsky set out to crush the men whom, four years before, he had so admired. His Red Army attacked across the slippery, crumbling ice. The soldiers suffered fearsome losses, but at last they stormed onto the island and destroyed the rebels.

Lenin had already decided that there must be a change of course. Communism, it seemed, was pushing ahead too fast, making new enemies and failing to produce the promised

Some judgements on Lenin

Lenin was Bolshevism, and Bolshevism was Lenin. Rarely in modern times has a man so strongly impressed his own individuality upon a movement of astounding extent and still incalculable consequences . . . This short, bald-headed, snub-nosed man set himself to the task of making the restless masses of the Russian people the centre and starting-point of a great world upheaval . . . Lenin did not hesitate for a single instant to revive the worst traditions of despotism.

The Times, 23 January 1924

Lenin symbolises the Russian Revolution as a movement of the poor and oppressed . . . who have successfully risen against the great and the powerful . . . Lenin stands for all those qualities – purposefulness, realism, common sense, will-power, pugnacity – which were most conspicuously lacking in the pre-revolutionary intelligentsia.

C.P. Hill, *Lenin and the Russian Revolution*, 1947

. . . I was now curious to see the face of the man who had deliberately contrived the use of millions of human beings as guinea-pigs in a gigantic laboratory. I had read the letters he wrote from Germany in 1916, where, following Marx, he declared his belief that a successful Communist revolution could be made only in a highly industrialized country, and that Russia was in no way ready for it. . . . Lenin cared not at all for the people or the improvement in their condition, but only for his theories and the power to try them out. . . . In my view the man was a monster.

Elisaveta Fen, in her autobiography *Remember Russia 1915–25*

If Lenin had died young, the tightly centralised Bolshevik Party could scarcely have emerged. If he had dropped dead in Zurich in March 1917, the Bolsheviks would not have moved into a position of total hostility to the other socialist and democratic parties. If he had died in July or August 1917, they would not have seized power. If he had died in the early months of 1918, they would not have signed the Treaty of Brest-Litovsk, and could have fallen . . . If he had died under Fanny Kaplan's bullets in August 1918, they would most probably have lost the Civil War. But for his insistence they would almost certainly not have switched to the New Economic Policy in 1921, and this would probably have meant their collapse . . . And, but for his insistence, the Communist International might not have been formed.

R. Conquest, *Lenin*, 1972

It was Lenin, flying in the face of the elements . . . who put forward and defended bold and innovative views . . . The generations of Soviet people living now could not conceive of their lives today without Lenin's greatest achievement – the October Revolution. For the October Revolution is the might and the glory of the homeland, our way of life and our plans.

A modern Soviet view in *Soviet Union*, April 1980

4   Stalin's revolution: building a new Russia

The struggle for power

When Lenin died, the Party he had created controlled the whole former Tsarist Empire, except for the Baltic coastlands and Poland. In 1922 that empire was reorganised as the Union of Soviet Socialist Republics (USSR), made up of at first four, and later fifteen, republics. Each had its own government and Party, but all came under Moscow's authority. Throughout the Soviet Union, in every village, factory, town, province and republic, the elected soviet was led by Party members and guided by the local Party committee.

Party members looked back with pride to Lenin's revolution, but their leaders knew that the real revolution was yet to come. They had changed Russia's government, but had yet to

The pyramid of power: State and Party

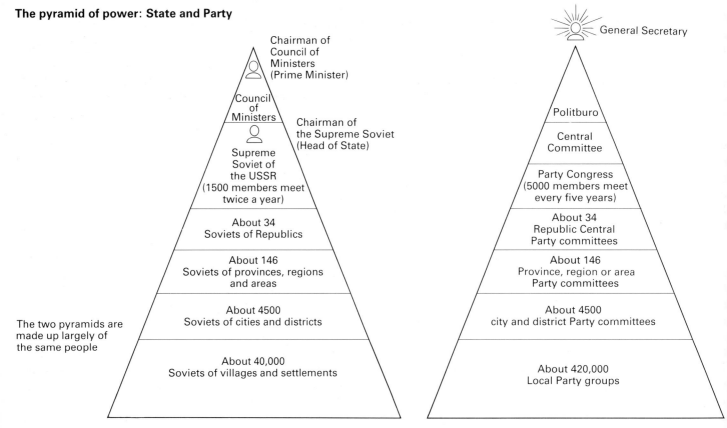

The two pyramids are made up largely of the same people

Chairman of Council of Ministers (Prime Minister)

Council of Ministers

Chairman of the Supreme Soviet (Head of State)

Supreme Soviet of the USSR (1500 members meet twice a year)

About 34 Soviets of Republics

About 146 Soviets of provinces, regions and areas

About 4500 Soviets of cities and districts

About 40,000 Soviets of villages and settlements

General Secretary

Politburo

Central Committee

Party Congress (5000 members meet every five years)

About 34 Republic Central Party committees

About 146 Province, region or area Party committees

About 4500 city and district Party committees

About 420,000 Local Party groups

change Russia's way of life to fit their socialist beliefs. They wanted work and profits shared equally; greedy capitalists would exploit the workers no more. They also wanted to bring their country up-to-date, to use modern technology and industry to improve standards of living. 'Communism is soviet power plus electrification,' said Lenin. 'The old Russia of primitive lighting and a crust of black bread is going to be covered by a network of electricity stations,' promised Bukharin. Immensely hard work and much money would be needed to provide machinery, factories, power stations and trained workers. The foundations had been laid in Tsarist times with foreign help, but Communists could expect little help from a fearful capitalist world.

Each of the men who had worked closely with Lenin had his own ideas of how to strengthen socialism and modernise the Soviet Union. They had seen their leader change policies to suit circumstances, like abandoning War Communism for the NEP. With Lenin gone, each argued his own plans and each distrusted the others. Their disagreements made it possible for one to become dictator.

Zinoviev had been Lenin's closest ally. He was President of the Comintern – leader of world Communism. Kamenev, who ran the Moscow Party, faithfully supported him. But Trotsky, vigorous, ruthless and eloquent, seemed much more a true leader. 'The most able person in the Central Committee,' wrote Lenin in his last advice to his successors, 'he has too much self-confidence'. Trotsky's name was known and feared around the world, as hero (or villain) of the Revolution and creator of the Red Army. Of younger men, Lenin thought Bukharin the ablest, 'a most valuable and distinguished thinker'.

Zinoviev could count on his colleagues to unite against Trotsky, because they feared him as a possible 'Napoleon', ambitious for sole power. Zinoviev's best ally was Stalin, a hard worker to whom Lenin had entrusted important jobs. In the government, Stalin was Commissar for Nationalities, responsible for the non-Russian half of the population, as well as Commissar for State Control, which put him in charge of local soviets and local commissars all over the Soviet Union. In the Party, he ran the 'Orgburo', which organised membership. Because he was good at administrative work, which the others thought dull, he was given another job in 1922 as Secretary General of the Party. Lenin was beginning to

Stalin had this photograph widely reproduced to show Lenin's trust in his faithful friend and follower. It was taken in 1922, soon after Stalin had become General Secretary and while Lenin was recovering from his first stroke. Later, Lenin came to distrust Stalin.

wonder whether Stalin was not gathering too much power, and in his last advice he warned, 'Stalin is too rude . . . I propose to the comrades that they should consider a means of removing Stalin . . . to prevent a split'. But Stalin's comrades failed to do so. So while Trotsky, Zinoviev and Bukharin, well-known men of ideas and ability, argued about Communism's future, Stalin quietly remoulded the Party to suit himself.

Many saw Stalin as more reliable and practical than the others. Those who thought less highly of him found themselves left out of meetings, sacked from their posts, even expelled from the Party; the Secretary General, after all, appointed local Party officials, and the Orgburo decided membership. Stalin also played off one ambitious leader against another. First, he helped Zinoviev and Kamenev to outwit Trotsky, who was urging world revolution and calling for shock brigades of workers to transform Soviet industry. Then he joined Bukharin to oppose Zinoviev and Kamenev, leaders of the left of the Party who favoured ending the NEP and working for true socialism. Finally, he turned on Bukharin, champion of the NEP and leader of the right, who favoured a more humane form of socialism. By 1926 Stalin was foremost among the leaders, and over the next three years his rivals were driven from Politburo and Party. Since the Party had decided in 1921 that there were to be no disagreements, Stalin made sure that no one who argued with him remained a Party member.

By 1929 Stalin was unchallenged as Lenin's heir. He kept no post in government, but his job as Party Secretary General made him the real ruler of the Soviet Union; in practice he was dictator. Now he set out to transform the country.

Industrial revolution: the Five-year Plans

Stalin's way ahead was decided partly by the arguments he used in the leadership disputes. Trotsky had wanted speedy world revolution; Stalin countered that it was better to strengthen the Soviet Union first, to 'build Socialism in one country'. Bukharin had argued that continuation of NEP freedom would encourage farmers and workers to produce more, building up wealth to pay for new machinery, power and transport. Stalin replied that the NEP had played its part and must end, so that the country might advance towards true socialism.

The NEP had restored some prosperity, and peasants were unlikely to welcome government or Party interference. But in 1917 Lenin's sharp blow had won power for the small group of Bolsheviks; similar drive and determination now could make another revolution. 'Our task is not to study economics but to change it,' said one of Stalin's supporters in 1927. 'There are no fortresses which Bolsheviks cannot storm.' Instead of facing Russian realities, the Communists proposed re-shaping realities to fit their theories.

By 1926, under the NEP, industrial production had generally recovered to pre-war levels, though nowhere near what it might have been without war, revolution and civil war. Stalin was convinced that state interference could speed up indust-

The Turksib (Turkestan-Siberian) Railway, begun in Tsarist times to link Central Asia to the Trans-Siberian, was opened in 1929–30 as one of the first achievements of the drive for industrialisation. A highly decorated locomotive passes under a ceremonial arch.

rial growth. In 1928 he announced a Five-year Plan for development, setting every industry a target for production. In 1929 all the targets were raised. Industrial output was to rise by 180 per cent. Coal and oil production must double, iron and steel increase threefold. Everyone had to work harder, longer hours.

And they did. Many were inspired by the thought of making the Soviet Union rich and strong by their own efforts, guided by Stalin and the Party. They were encouraged constantly by posters, radio, newspapers, films and Party officials. Moreover, they knew that slackness might mean facing accusations of treachery or sabotage.

Sometimes there were muddles. Knowing the penalties for failure, factory managers pushed workers till they dropped, produced shoddy goods, or 'cooked' the figures to prove success. Goods left out of the plan were not made, however much they were needed; but anything in the plan had to be made, whether needed or not. Absenteeism led to swift dis-

А 1934 poster shows skilled women at work, and calls for new technology to build socialism.

already brought industry to the point where it was about to 'take off' into rapid growth anyway, so that similar results might have followed with less waste and suffering. The Soviet Union was going through an industrial revolution, as Britain had a century earlier; and the workers were going through similar hardships. Nevertheless, the Soviet people were left with a sense of triumph, convinced that through their own efforts they were catching up with the west. They had set up a base for future industrial growth at a time when the capitalist world was suffering from economic depression and unemployment.

Spectacular schemes that could only have been started by a powerful government showed off the success of socialism. The huge Dnepropetrovsk dam supplied electricity for Ukrainian industry, the 'Turksib' Railway opened up much of central Asia, the White Sea–Baltic–Volga Canals linked Soviet waterways. Foreign visitors especially admired Moscow's new underground railway with its palatial marble stations; the Moscow Party Secretary who directed its construction was the former steelworker Nikita Khrushchev, now a loud supporter of Stalin. But much heavy work in all these enterprises was done by political prisoners being 're-educated' by hard labour.

The Five-year Plan seemed to have transformed the Soviet Union. No sooner was it completed than Stalin launched another; and later, plan after plan set new targets for growth. Each was acclaimed a success. If there were muddles, failures or waste, the Party rarely admitted it.

Yet despite apparent success, the first plans made conditions no better for most workers than they had been under the Tsars. There was no more housing, food or clothing to meet immediate needs. Working conditions were in many ways harsher than ever. But in other ways life was, as Stalin said, better for workers and their families, for now the State provided schools, paid holidays, pensions and medical care. By 1940 the USSR had a higher proportion of doctors than most western countries.

Agrarian revolution: collectivisation

Though industry was growing, agriculture was still by far the largest sector of the Soviet economy. Farming methods remained backward, despite the efforts of Stolypin in the 1900s, and progress under the NEP. Stalin well knew that farmers

missal, and strikes were forbidden. One worker, Alexei Stakhanov, who on one shift in 1935 mined fourteen times as much coal as his target, became a national hero, and all workers were urged to copy him.

The hardship and effort paid off. Industrial production rose impressively, though not to the level demanded by the Plan. Perhaps the success was as a result of Stalin's guidance and pressure; but some economists argue that the NEP had

Women of a minority nationality in the Caucasus in 1929, learning to read and write. The Communists conducted a vigorous campaign for peasant literacy, for all must read and understand government propaganda.

were not interested in building socialism. Instead of supplying cheap food for industrial workers, they hoarded it to push up prices. In 1928 the government had to seize by force the grain it needed. Further, Stalin and his Party supporters were alarmed by the growing importance of prosperous peasants. Successful kulaks were influential in their villages, and that upset local Party secretaries, who saw their own leadership threatened.

In 1929 Stalin announced that peasants should all join 'Collective Farms':

> Can Soviet power and the work of building socialism rest for long on two different foundations: on large-scale, intensive socialist industry and scattered, backward small-scale peas-

ant farming? No, the *socialist* way is to introduce large collective farms, using machinery and scientific methods.

The *kolkhoz* would be directed and inspired by good Party members, and would teach farmers to work together progressively. This would be true socialism. It would bring the vast increase of farm production that the Soviet Union needed. There would be cheap food for all, and capital to finance Soviet industry. And it would end the power of the 'NEP men' and the greed of the kulaks.

The Communists had become over-confident, believing that they had only to decree change to make it happen. They had done nothing to prepare for this revolutionary development, or to plan the new collectives. They met stubborn opposition. After doing so well under the NEP most farmers could not see why they should give up independence, land, cattle and pigs to share with others and take orders from a Party official. They resented keen young townspeople telling them how to run their own villages. The richest peasants, the kulaks, naturally led the resistance.

Stalin tried to sidestep the problem. There must be no violence, he declared. Peasants should join collectives of their own free will. At the same time Party officials had to make sure that all did join, and they could only do so by sending armed men into the villages. When this happened peasants refused to plant crops on land they would soon lose; they slaughtered their livestock and feasted rather than hand over their property.

Stalin paused a moment. In March 1930 he called a halt to collectivisation, fearing there might be no harvest at all. Peasants took back their land, planted and harvested; then they found collectivisation going ahead more forcefully than ever. Kulaks, and everyone resisting Party orders, were denounced as enemies of the workers, the Party and the Revolution. Such people were rarely given a chance to join a kolkhoz. Instead, their land, houses and stock were seized, and whole families were herded off to Siberia. Millions of men, women and children died from starvation, disease, cold or ill-treatment in, or on the way to, the harsher parts of that country. Sometimes peasants fought back; then troops and State Security Police (NKVD) surrounded and wiped out whole villages.

Peasants might be forced into collectives, but they could not

Collective farmers were not trusted to run their own machinery, and tractors like this 1937 model were hired out from Machine and Tractor Stations set up all over the country.

be forced to produce. The grain harvest, 85 million tonnes in 1930, fell to 71 million in 1931. The 70 million cattle of 1928 had dropped to 38 million by 1933, the 26 million pigs to 12 million. Much food was seized for industrial workers, leaving starvation in the rich farmlands of European Russia. Millions more died; no one knows how many. It was an appalling disaster.

Stalin had imposed socialism in the countryside and ended the influence of the NEP men, but he had not won the increased production he expected. Food output did not recover for many years, until collective farmers were allowed small private plots for themselves. Methods remained backward and, though foundations had been laid for progress, Soviet agriculture remained less productive than that of the west.

From Stalin's point of view, it hardly mattered that living conditions in the countryside remained miserable. The Party's hold was now absolute in rural Russia. For good Communists,

collectivisation was a triumph, and it still is. In 1980 Leonid Brezhnev summed up its importance:

> From the *political* standpoint that system has strengthened the Soviet state . . . from the *economic* angle, the collective farm system has placed the advantages of large-scale farming at the service of socialism and communism and enabled agriculture to develop on a modern industrial basis; from the *social* viewpoint, it has freed the peasants from exploitation and poverty.

Dictator

Stalin had pushed through his revolution. He had shown iron will and used powerful weapons: the Party, with its rigid discipline; the state-controlled press and radio; and the NKVD. Of course the hardships and brutality brought complaints; and (though Stalin would not admit it) the results were not as splendid as promised. Some things had gone badly wrong.

Stalin was suspicious. Who was to blame for these upsets? Capitalist countries resented the success of the new socialist state, and perhaps had agents inside the USSR. From time to time foreign engineers working in the Soviet Union, or officials whose departments had failed, were put on trial as wreckers and saboteurs. Usually they were expelled, imprisoned or shot.

Perhaps, Stalin feared, some Party members were secretly working against him. Certainly many were appalled by the violence. Stalin's own wife was so horrified that she committed suicide in 1932. Others looked to alternative leaders: to Bukharin, who believed in a more liberal and humane form of communism but had none of Stalin's ruthless ability to command; or to Sergei Kirov, the up-and-coming Party boss in Leningrad (once St Petersburg and Petrograd).

Stalin felt threatened. If his revolution was to last, the Party must be reliable. Not only those who opposed his policies, but any who failed to back them energetically enough, must go. So began the great purge, the Great Terror, when Stalin's supposed enemies in the Party and throughout the USSR were destroyed.

In December 1934 Kirov was assassinated. Perhaps Stalin himself arranged the murder of this potential rival. At any rate, he used the opportunity to throw blame on everyone he

The Great Purge

Stalin killed:

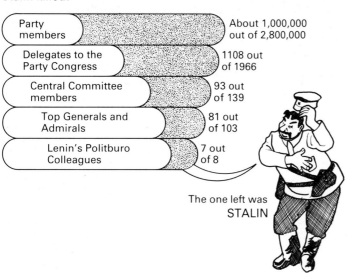

Party members	About 1,000,000 out of 2,800,000
Delegates to the Party Congress	1108 out of 1966
Central Committee members	93 out of 139
Top Generals and Admirals	81 out of 103
Lenin's Politburo Colleagues	7 out of 8

The one left was STALIN

distrusted or disliked. Over the next four years all Stalin's suspected enemies or lukewarm supporters were imprisoned, sent to dreadful labour camps from which they never returned, or shot. Show trials were staged for some, especially for old rivals like Zinoviev and Bukharin. With much publicity they were accused of long-standing treachery to the Party, the Soviet Union and Stalin. Usually they confessed. Perhaps some really had hoped to remove Stalin; others believed they could best serve their Party by admitting guilt. Most were tricked, threatened or tortured into confession.

As well as untrustworthy Party members, Stalin and his NKVD 'liquidated' many leading figures from every side of Soviet life: army and navy officers, engineers and industrial managers, university professors, leading writers and artists. No one suspected of less than total loyalty could be trusted in any position of influence. Most simply disappeared, to be shot or sent to labour camps; and when top people disappeared, so did their families, colleagues and helpers. By 1939 it is thought there were 9 million prisoners, while 3 million had been killed. No one can be sure of the figures. More than half of the 2,000 delegates at the 1934 Party Congress were later shot; so were 110 out of 139 members of the Party's Central Committee. Fifteen former members of the Politburo were murdered, and

others died in dubious circumstances. Kirov had already been assassinated, and Trotsky was murdered in exile in 1940. 'Stalin was a very distrustful man, sickly suspicious . . . Everywhere and in everything he saw "enemies", "two facers" and "spies",' said Khrushchev much later. But at the time Khrushchev survived by supporting Stalin in denouncing 'wreckers, spies and murderers':

> Those miserable pigmies wanted to destroy the unity of the Party and the Soviet State. They raised treacherous hands against Comrade Stalin – Stalin, our hope; Stalin, our desire; Stalin, the light of advanced and progressive mankind; Stalin, our will; Stalin, our victory.

The Terror was at its worst from 1936 to 1939. It remained an important weapon of government until Stalin's death in 1953. Terror bred terror; one way to prove loyalty was to accuse others of treachery, while the NKVD was zealous to show its enthusiasm and efficiency. Yet most Russians probably went on believing that Stalin was wise, all-seeing, and had their real interests at heart; that they were co-operating in building a new society. Once, Russian peasants had felt much the same about the Tsar, their 'Little Father'.

Stalin had much more effective propaganda, censorship and police. Where Tsarism had tried to stop people speaking against the system, communism insisted that everyone must work for it. Artists, novelists and composers whose work did not satisfy the rulers found themselves jobless, or pushed into labour camps. Writers slavishly copied Stalin's stilted and clumsy Russian style (Stalin was Georgian). Artists painted the simple realistic pictures he liked; musicians used the popular tunes he fancied, and composed songs in praise of Soviet progress and their leader. Film-makers turned from glorifying the Revolution to showing heroic Russian leaders, past and present. History was rewritten: Trotsky was left out of the story of the Revolution, and even removed from old photographs. Going further back, historians revised their ideas about some tsars, and textbooks praised such rulers as Ivan the Terrible and Peter the Great. One wrote of Ivan's 'ability and foresight . . . He mapped out the country's aims and tasks with wisdom and profound judgement and pursued them doggedly and indefatigably . . . Under him Russia became a united, powerful state.' They were really thinking not of the old tsar but of Stalin.

The arts under Stalin

The director Eisenstein set out to make a three-part film about Tsar Ivan the Terrible. Part I (made in 1944) showed him as a stern and wise ruler, as here. Stalin approved. Part II (in 1945) suggested Ivan could be cruel as well. Stalin took offence. The film was banned, and Eisenstein died of a heart attack before he could make Part III.

Stalinist architecture favoured massive size, towers and pinnacles, and rich decoration. The University of Moscow was built during Stalin's last years.

In An Unforgettable Encounter a Soviet artist showed the thrill ordinary people were supposed to feel on meeting the great and good Stalin, surrounded by his faithful colleagues, including Khrushchev.

The Great Patriotic War, 1941–45

While they were building 'Socialism in one country', Russia's Communists did little to encourage revolution outside the Soviet Union. Most Soviet citizens, anyway, were allowed no foreign contacts. The Comintern linked Communist parties in many lands; these parties spread news of splendid progress in the Soviet Union, sometimes took part in democratic politics, or tried to take over trade unions. Usually they were given encouragement and a little cash by Moscow, but no more. Stalin left such active Communists as those in China to carry out revolution in their own way, preferring to keep on friendly terms with their powerful opponent, Chiang Kai-Shek. He sent some help to the Republican side (Communists and Socialists) fighting in the Spanish Civil War of 1936–9, but far less than Germany and Italy supplied to General Franco. He sought co-operation with the western democracies against Nazi Germany, but Britain and France distrusted his intentions and came to terms with Hitler, sacrificing Czechoslovakia, in 1938.

Deciding that the western powers were no good as allies, and suspecting that they hoped to turn Hitler's war-like ambitions eastwards, Stalin agreed to a Non-aggression Pact with Germany in August 1939. This meant that Germany was free to fight Poland, France and Britain without Soviet interference, so that the USSR's main enemies would be heavily engaged. The USSR and Germany partitioned and occupied Poland, and Stalin used the opportunity to seize other lands on the Soviet borders. Estonia, Latvia and Lithuania, once parts of the Tsar's empire, were re-occupied in 1940, while Bessarabia (Moldavia) was taken from Romania. But a Soviet attack late in 1939 on another of the Tsar's former territories, Finland, met fierce resistance. Partly because so many officers had been purged, the Soviet army was not fit to fight, and suffered disastrously. The Finns kept their independence; but, faced with overwhelming numbers, they agreed to give up some territory.

Stalin thought he was safeguarding his frontiers as well as recovering Russia's former empire. But in 1941, having mastered most of western Europe, Hitler turned against his real enemy, the Soviet Union. He despised Communism as a debased political creed, and Slavs as an inferior race; and he sought German living-space in the rich Ukrainian farmlands.

Stalin, blindly over-confident, was taken completely by surprise. The German invasion rolled forward. Though five-year plans had provided aeroplanes, tanks and guns, the Red Army handled them ineffectively, while many people actually welcomed the Germans as liberators. It was nearly two weeks before Stalin dared speak on the radio to his people. When he did, he appealed to them as 'Comrades, brothers and sisters, my friends', calling on all who loved their country to stand with him against Fascist invaders, cowards and traitors.

The Soviet armies suffered terrible disasters, but some survived. As the Germans pushed towards Moscow they found resistance stiffening. Nazi brutality turned many, who had at first welcomed the Germans, fiercely against them. Their lines of communication were long and awkward; mud, snow and bitter cold made conditions very difficult. At last the German army was checked and thrown back. In the winter of 1942–3 Hitler's and Stalin's armies fought their most desperate battle in the ruins of Stalingrad, whose very name attracted both leaders to it.

Surviving Russians rallied round Stalin, who posed as a heroic and patriotic leader. He was no military genius, but he was dogged and ruthless. He moved Soviet arms industries eastwards, behind the Urals. He shot generals who showed weakness. He sent to Siberia the families of those who surrendered, and whole Soviet peoples (like the Crimean Tartars) accused of helping the Germans. At the same time the pressure for revolutionary socialism was dropped, and old-fashioned patriotism was encouraged. Even the Church, previously persecuted, was allowed freedom to preach against the invaders. In the army, Stalin restored the old Tsarist ranks, and smart uniforms with epaulettes and decorations in place of drabness. To prove to his new capitalist allies that the Soviet Union was no longer trying to overthrow them, he dissolved the Comintern. He dropped the *Internationale*, the USSR's Communist hymn, in favour of a patriotic Russian marching tune.

For four years the struggle brought hardship, misery and massive casualties. In the end, Stalin's ruthless leadership helped to save the USSR and bring victory. The Soviet people, those not in exile or labour camps, rejoiced and praised their leader for his foresight, courage and skill. Those who, like Khrushchev, knew that Stalin was also to blame for the military disasters and hardships of 1941, kept quiet.

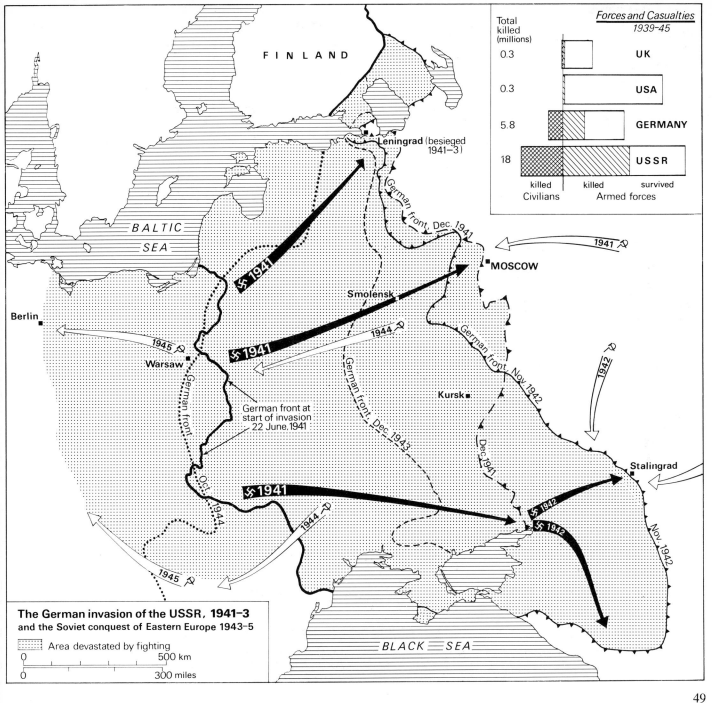

FINLAND

BALTIC
SEA

Leningrad (besieged 1941–3)

German front, Dec. 1941

MOSCOW

1941

Smolensk

Berlin

1945 ☭

1944 ☭

Warsaw

1941

German front at start of invasion 22 June, 1941

German front, Dec. 1943

Kursk

German front, Nov. 1942

1942

Oct. 1944

Dec. 1941

1941

1944 ☭

Stalingrad

1942

1942

Nov. 1942

1945 ☭

BLACK SEA

The German invasion of the USSR, 1941–3
and the Soviet conquest of Eastern Europe 1943–5

Area devastated by fighting

0   500 km

0   300 miles

Forces and Casualties 1939–45

Total killed (millions)			
0.3			UK
0.3			USA
5.8			GERMANY
18			USSR

killed Civilians | killed | survived Armed forces

Stalin's last years

After the war, the USSR, despite enormous losses, was politically in a very powerful position. The Red Army occupied eastern Europe and half of defeated Germany. Russia kept control of this area by setting up Communist governments that took orders from Moscow. In Poland, for example, traditionally hostile to Russia, a pro-Communist 'Committee of National Liberation' was set up. Other Polish leaders, invited to Moscow for talks, vanished into prison. This policy created a buffer zone in case the capitalist powers decided to use their might (which now included the atomic bomb) against the USSR.

The USA and other democracies complained of the Communists' brutal methods in the east European satellites, and even before the end of the war against Germany a new Cold War was developing between East and West. By 1946 Churchill was speaking of an 'Iron Curtain' dividing Europe and Soviet leaders were denouncing US imperialism. What the Communists saw as a danger led them to impose ever tighter controls. Any opponents in the satellite countries were purged, with show trials like those Moscow had seen in the 1930s.

Within the Soviet Union, Communist policies were imposed as harshly as ever. Former prisoners of war, and many soldiers who had seen and perhaps liked the outside world, were shut away in labour camps. Anyone showing admiration for western ways, or insufficient enthusiasm for socialism, was in danger. When the new state of Israel came into being in 1948, for example, Soviet Jews were suspected of divided loyalty; many were arrested and some shot. The collective farm system was tightened up, and peasants trying to profit from their private plots were heavily taxed. Once more writers, artists and musicians had to support the Party line and glorify Stalin.

Stalin was ageing, but he was still formidable. Early in 1953 he began preparing a new purge. He was worried by the ambitions of those who hoped to succeed him. People like the foreign minister Molotov, and police chief Beria, who had risen as Stalin's henchmen during the purges in the 1930s, began to fear that Stalin might turn on them. They were saved by his sudden death in March 1953.

Under Stalin, the USSR had become a superpower, passing

The Soviet Union in Eastern Europe

.... Frontiers in 1938
———— Frontiers in 1946
═══ The Iron Curtain 1946
▒▒▒ Occupied by USSR 1940
░░░ Occupied by USSR 1945
<u>YUGOSLAVIA</u> Satellite states; dates show
1948   resistance to Soviet control

0 — 500 km
0 — 300 miles

FINLAND

ESTONIA

LATVIA

LITHUANIA

EAST
PRUSSIA

SOVIET

BELORUSSIA

UNION

WEST
GERMANY

EAST
GERMANY
1953

<u>POLAND</u>
1956, 1981

GERMANY

CZECHOSLOVAKIA
1968

UKRAINE

AUSTRIA

<u>HUNGARY</u>
1956

MOLDAVIA

<u>ROMANIA</u>
1970s

ITALY

<u>YUGOSLAVIA</u>
1948

<u>BULGARIA</u>

<u>ALBANIA</u>
1961

GREECE

TURKEY

from isolation to a dominating role in world affairs. Stalin had bullied and lied and murdered, dragooning the many peoples and vast lands of the Soviet Union, crushing all who got in his way. His revolution, some thought, had complemented Lenin's, giving the Soviet people and the whole world hope for a better future. Others, though, felt he had destroyed Lenin's work, abandoning revolutionary ideals and restoring the worst evils of Tsarism in an intensified form: brutality, political persecution, bureaucracy, censorship and imperialist oppression.

Stalin's preserved body joined that of Lenin in the Red Square mausoleum. He too was revered as saint and founding-father of Soviet Communism; but not for long.

The Iron Curtain:
the view from opposite sides

An iron curtain has descended across the continent. Behind that line lie all the capitals of the ancient states of Central and Eastern Europe . . . All these famous cities, and the populations around them . . . are subject not only to Soviet influence, but to a very high and increasing measure of control from Moscow . . . The Communist parties . . . have been raised to power far beyond their numbers, and are seeking everywhere to obtain totalitarian control. Police governments are prevailing in nearly every case, and so far . . . there is no true democracy.

Winston Churchill, Fulton, Missouri, March 1946

The reactionary imperialist elements all over the world, notably in Britain, America and France, had reposed great hopes in Hitler's Germany . . . as a force most capable of inflicting a blow on the Soviet Union, to destroy or weaken and undermine its influence . . . But their hopes were not realised. The Soviet Union and the freedom-loving nations proved stronger than the imperialists had expected . . . America's aspirations to world supremacy encounter an obstacle in the USSR . . . Alarmed by the achievements of Socialism in the USSR, the American reactionaries want to take upon themselves the mission of 'saviours' of the capitalist system.

Andrei Zhdanov, Speech to the Cominform, September 1947

5   The legacy of revolution: Khrushchev to Gorbachev

The Soviet people mourned Stalin, some of them with real sincerity. Many felt lost without the firm hand that had moulded their lives. At the same time there was enormous relief, and hope that life might become easier. But Stalin's supporters were still in control, men who had risen by serving him, and dared not allow his Party to be displaced. The moment Stalin died, they placed the police and army on alert for trouble. But Stalin had destroyed opposition so effectively that the only real danger came from disputes within the leadership itself.

Successive revolutions over thirty-six years left Stalin's heirs with immense power and problems. The new leaders had to guide a troubled superpower, created by revolution, ideology, terror, dictatorship and war, towards peace, stability and prosperity.

Khrushchev

The Party remained firmly in control. The leaders nearly doubled membership in the decade after Stalin's death. This was still only one Soviet citizen in twelve, but the Party claimed to include all the most active, educated and public-spirited people, and to provide leadership in every kind of activity. In 1977 a new Soviet Constitution detailed the key part of the Communist Party in all state bodies.

At the summit, the Party hoped to replace the dead dictator with a 'collective leadership'. It was not to be. Once again, suspicions and ambitions led to a single leader. At Stalin's death three men stood out: Molotov, his loyal henchman since 1917; Beria, his powerful police chief; and Malenkov, his closest supporter, who took over as Prime Minister and Party Secretary. They agreed that the ruthless ways of Stalin must be modified, but they disagreed about the speed and scope of change; and they were very suspicious of one another. Within a week the others forced Malenkov to pass over his Secretary-ship to Khrushchev. Soon after, alarmed by Beria's sweeping plans for swift reform, his colleagues had him shot. Molotov, suspected of being too attached to Stalin's memory and methods, sensibly kept quiet.

It was Nikita Khrushchev, the forceful ex-steelworker, who came to the top. His rise showed that the Party Secretaryship was still the key post, though he took the title 'First Secretary', not (like Stalin) 'General Secretary'. Khrushchev never copied Stalin's tyranny or enjoyed the same control. There were still struggles for power, and in 1957 leading opponents even attempted to remove him. The First Secretary outwitted them with help from ordinary Party members and from the army, headed by the war hero Marshal Zhukov. Unlike Stalin, he did not kill his defeated rivals. Instead they were expelled from the Politburo: Malenkov was sent to manage a power station in Central Asia, while Molotov became ambassador to Mongolia.

For seven years Khrushchev led the Soviet Union in his own erratic way. He was very different from the cold, remote Stalin; he was lively, shrewd, and quick-tempered. In earthy peasant language, he questioned, argued, bullied and joked with workers, Party officials or foreign statesmen. He had kept quiet under Stalin. Now he enjoyed saying what he pleased. He ruled by instinct rather than reason, ignoring committees and paperwork. He produced bright ideas and instant solutions, riding roughshod over cautious critics to try out his schemes. Sometimes they turned out disastrously.

A thaw

As Khrushchev and his rivals jockeyed for power, they argued over how to deal with the problems left by Russia's revolutions. Should they end the Cold War and seek understanding with the capitalist world? Should they end the labour camps and free millions of prisoners? Should they allow more free-

Khrushchev (1894–1971) enjoyed travelling, meeting people, and being photographed. Here he is on a visit to the USA in 1959, when his openness and common sense dispelled much of the suspicion built up in Stalin's time.

dom of speech and political activity? How could they achieve economic growth? Could they raise living standards by producing food and consumer goods in place of heavy machinery?

Everyone agreed that Stalin's harsh policies must be eased. They cut prices, allowing people to buy more; but that caused severe shortages. They eased political and military control over eastern Europe; but that gave people who had suffered silently under Stalin their chance to protest, so that just three months after his death an uprising broke out in East Germany. Friendly moves towards the USA met only with cold rebuff from a suspicious President Eisenhower and his Secretary of State, John Foster Dulles.

Despite such setbacks, Khrushchev and his colleagues pushed ahead to rid the USSR of the effects of Stalinism. Censorship was relaxed a little, so that officials (but not Party leaders) might be criticised. The power of the security police was reduced, and it was run by a committee, the KGB, instead of by a minister. The army was kept under Party control, and Khrushchev even sacked his ally, Zhukov, when he appeared too ambitious. Millions of political prisoners were released from the camps.

As Stalin's surviving victims reappeared and enjoyed some freedom to speak out, complaint and criticism grew. Intellectual life in the Soviet Union seemed to awaken after a long sleep. In 1954 the novelist Ilya Ehrenburg welcomed the new freedom in *The Thaw*. Later, in 1962, a returned prisoner named Alexander Solzhenitsyn described the horrifying life of the labour camps in *One Day in the Life of Ivan Denisovich*, telling of things that before had been mentioned only in whispers.

The attack on Stalin

As such stories circulated, Khrushchev decided it was safest to direct the complaints against Stalin. He must make it clear that it was one evil man at fault, and not the Communist Party. In February 1956, when the 20th Party Congress met, he delivered a four-hour attack on his old master. Officially the speech was secret, but copies went to Party branches, and soon everyone knew that Communism's revered former leader was under attack. The successor of Marx and Lenin, Russia's guide in building socialism, was now denounced as a murderous megalomaniac. He had, said Khrushchev, shown 'his intolerance, his brutality and his abuse of power'.

The 'Secret Speech' upset many faithful Communists, and helped to cause unrest in eastern Europe, especially in Hungary and Poland. If the worst tales told about the revolutionary regime by its enemies were really true, and Communists had lied to conceal that truth, who could trust a Communist? Could such misrule have happened without revolution and Party dictatorship? Was this sort of tyranny the inevitable outcome of Lenin's revolution? Outside the Soviet Union, many Communists left the Party in disgust. Khrushchev's own colleagues feared he had said too much.

Khrushchev went on blaming Stalin for all that was wrong, so that Lenin, his Party and his Revolution could remain beyond criticism. Stalin's preserved body lost its place alongside Lenin's, and the many towns named in his honour were renamed; Stalingrad (once Tsaritsyn) now became Volgograd.

Making Communism work

Despite the upheaval, the Party had not weakened in its determination to build a Communist society. All workers should contribute what they could to the community, and in turn the community would meet all needs. The Party had not yet educated people away from selfishness; so it had to keep firm control to progress towards Communism, and to preserve the socialist system from its enemies.

But what did 'socialist' mean? In one sense, it meant any of Karl Marx's ideas that might be adapted and developed to suit the Soviet Union. Marx had made many statements which could be understood in different ways, and a clever Communist could use them to back any proposals. Stalin, it was said, used to decide his policy and leave his secretaries to fill his speeches with appropriate phrases from Marx and Lenin. Stalin had devised one pattern of socialism for the Soviet Union, and this pattern his successors kept.

Socialism benefited the Soviet people in many ways. They enjoyed free health care and medical treatment. Public transport was cheap and plentiful, and few private cars cluttered Soviet roads. Rents were low, though at first homes were grossly overcrowded; in Stalin's day two or three families crammed into each room. But Khrushchev began a massive house-building programme in the 1960s and by the 1980s most families had their own flat. Education was mostly free, with a wide range of schools setting a high standard of discipline and scholarship.

Socialism proved less successful in shaping the Soviet economy. Stalin had made it clear, in opposing Bukharin and ending the New Economic Policy, that there was to be no private enterprise. The State controlled industry and collectivised farming. Stalin's successors did not try to undo his revolution, but sought to run things more efficiently. The Five-year Plans continued. Output rose steadily, but centrally-controlled industry still suffered from muddle, bureaucracy and bottlenecks. In an attempt to solve these problems, Khrushchev abolished the Moscow ministries that planned all production, setting up instead a hundred regional economic councils. But this upset planners and officials and did not work well; each region tended to plan in competition with others rather than to meet consumer needs.

In agriculture, too, Khrushchev tried to boost output without destroying Stalin's system. He considered himself an expert and consequently did enormous damage. Impressed by the value of maize as a crop, he urged that it be planted widely, even where the climate guaranteed disastrous results. He made collectives buy and repair their own machinery, though they often proved incapable of doing so. Above all, Khrushchev discovered the 'Virgin Lands', forty million hectares of grassland in Central Asia. In 1954 thousands of young people were moved eastwards to plough and plant in Kazakhstan and Siberia. They suffered much hardship, but the plan was a huge initial success. In 1955 and after, the total grain harvest was 50 per cent greater than under Stalin, and for the first time regularly exceeded pre-revolutionary levels. But soon drought hit the 'Virgin Lands'. It became clear that the climate was not ideal, that cultivation turned the soil to dust, and that wasteful methods had been used for quick results. Production plummeted. It seemed that Khrushchev was no more successful than his predecessors in making socialist economics work on a grand scale.

The Soviet Union as a superpower

The Communists' early dreams of world revolution had long since faded. Stalin had cared only for strengthening the Soviet Union, even if it meant allying with Nazis or capitalists. After the defeat of Hitler, the Soviet Union dominated eastern Europe. What were the Soviet leaders' motives? Was it the old desire to spread revolution for the good of humanity? Was it to set up a buffer zone against possible attack from the West? Or was it old-fashioned Russian imperialism?

Stalin was certainly determined to regain those parts of the Tsar's empire lost in 1918, which meant seizing non-Russian nations such as the Baltic republics (Estonia, Latvia and Lithuania). The Russians maintained that these nations joined the Soviet Union freely, which was true in the sense that local Communists, the people who mattered in Soviet eyes, favoured such a union. But critics held that the Communists' treatment of non-Russians in the Soviet Union was more imperialist than that of the Tsars. Though paying lip-service to preserving national customs and arts, they kept Russian as the dominant language, and brought in Russians as technicians or farmers. Nomadic pastoralists were forcibly

Soviet nationalities. Kirghiz (above) and Latvians (right) pose in national dress. Such parades of colourful costume were encouraged to create a festive atmosphere, but any attempt to assert national interest was speedily suppressed until the days of glasnost.

settled and their steppes seized for agriculture; those resisting this destruction of their way of life – sometimes whole communities – were sent to Siberia. Moscow ruled, enforcing Moscow's policies. One outcome of Stalin's imperialism was the enthusiasm with which Ukrainians welcomed the German army in 1941, while Cossacks and Tartar soldiers deserted to fight beside the invaders. Whatever its motives, millions of people could testify that Russian imperialism was real and oppressive.

Still the Communist Party of the USSR claimed to be the foremost exponent of Marxist ideals, anxious to help and guide revolutionary groups everywhere, expecting support and obedience in return. Naturally, people who feared either Russian expansion or socialist revolution turned for help to the rival superpower, the USA. Power struggle was entangled inextricably with ideological clash in the Cold War.

The two great powers competed to win friends and influence governments, first in Europe, and later in Asia, Africa and Latin America. They competed by sending out propaganda, financial aid and technical experts. They competed to display their strength by building bigger and better nuclear weapons. They competed in space: in 1957 the Soviet Union proudly launched the first man-made satellite, and soon after showed how far ahead it was by photographing the hidden side of the moon and launching a man into space. But the USSR was poorer than the USA, and spending so much on weapons and space made it harder to improve living standards.

Khrushchev sought to avoid the dangers of rivalry. He wanted 'peaceful co-existence' between the superpowers so that they might compete in increasing prosperity and demonstrate whose system worked better. He had no doubt that ultimately socialism would succeed; 'We will bury you,' he announced cheerfully.

Khrushchev hurried along a peace settlement in Korea in 1953, and ended the occupation of Austria in 1955. He set off visiting around the world: Yugoslavia, China, India, western Europe and even, in 1959, the USA, where he scored a personal success. But he was exasperated by American suspicions and slowness to respond to his efforts. In 1960 an American U2 spy plane was caught over the Soviet Union. Khrushchev demanded an apology, and when he did not get it he wrecked a carefully arranged summit conference.

Shortly afterwards, Khrushchev gave whole-hearted support to the revolutionary government of Fidel Castro in Cuba, and in 1962 he started shipping nuclear missiles into Cuba, right on the US doorstep. The USA was alarmed and when President Kennedy struck back by blockading Cuba, the quarrel brought the world to the brink of war. Khrushchev realised he had underestimated American firmness, and quickly changed his policy. In 1963 the two superpowers concluded a Nuclear Test Ban Treaty, which checked the arms race and began the years of *détente*, or understanding, between Communist and capitalist camps.

Within the Communist-controlled world, Khrushchev's attack on Stalin and his moves towards co-existence brought division and unrest. China and Albania resented the 'betrayal' of Stalin's ideals. Other satellites expected freedom to follow their own paths to socialism, without orders from Moscow. The Chinese Communists had long disliked Moscow's domineering attitude, and when Khrushchev cut off Soviet help, the great Communist powers came near to blows. China's size and aggressiveness meant that Mao Zedong became a rival for leadership of the Communist world.

In eastern Europe, Khrushchev won back the friendship of Yugoslavia, where the leader Marshal Tito had quarrelled with Stalin. He drew the satellite countries into a new military alliance, the Warsaw Pact (1955), to face the West's NATO (North Atlantic Treaty Organisation) of 1949. But in Poland the Soviets had to accept a more liberal Communist leadership

October, 1956, Hungary: burning a Stalin portrait. The attack on Stalinism in the USSR encouraged Hungarian intellectuals and workers to oppose those whom Stalin had set in power over them. Street demonstrations built up into violence and revolution, which was only repressed by Soviet tanks.

under Gomulka when they realised that the Poles would strongly resist any Soviet invasion. In Hungary there was an upsurge of national feeling in 1956 which threatened to end Communist control. Khrushchev and his colleagues decided not to allow this. Soviet troops entered Budapest and crushed the Hungarian rebels in a few days of desperate fighting. As a demonstration of Soviet brutality and determination to keep satellite states obedient, the suppression of Hungary earned much hostility world-wide and alienated many Communist sympathisers.

Stability or stagnation? Khrushchev's successors

By 1964 Khrushchev had led the Party for eleven years. He had tried to undo some of the harmful effects of Russia's revolutions while preserving their successes. But he had blustered and blundered so much that those he had himself brought into the Politburo determined to get rid of him. They claimed he was too old, irresponsible and dictatorial, making moves such as the arming of Cuba and setting up regional economic organisations without consultation.

Khrushchev was overthrown without bloodshed. That in itself showed how much he had changed the methods of leadership since Stalin's day. It showed also how unchallenged was the power of the Party bosses, for there was no sign of protest. Khrushchev had made mistakes, and his successors tried to forget him. They re-wrote Soviet history to leave out his name. Many of his experiments were quickly abandoned. But he had shown that Communism need not be rigid and inhumane. He had left the Soviet Union a happier place than he found it. Moreover, by ending the Terror and improving living standards he had also eased Soviet relations with the West.

In Khrushchev's place the leaders wanted someone reliable and unexciting, who would not talk so much or make silly mistakes. As General Secretary they chose Leonid Brezhnev:

Leonid Brezhnev (1906–1982) on a poster dominating preparations for an October parade. Like his predecessors, Brezhnev was the object of a personality cult; his portrait was everywhere, his words were sacred, he could do no wrong. After his death, criticism soon followed.

The Soviet Union: government and economy

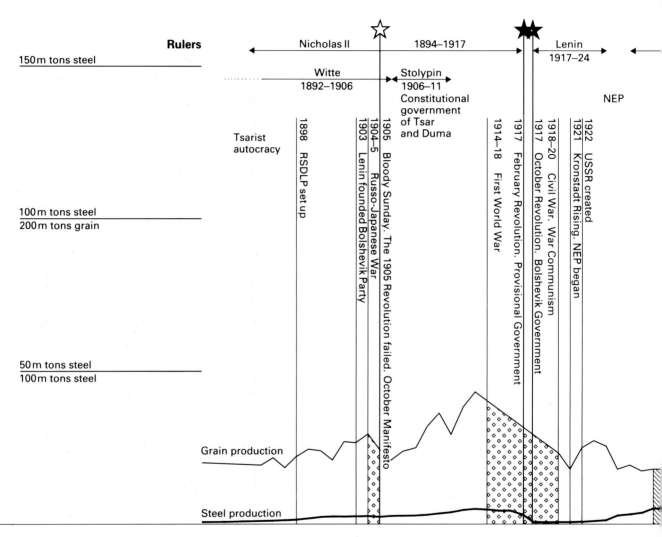

Rulers

150m tons steel

Nicholas II   1894–1917   Lenin 1917–24

Witte 1892–1906   Stolypin 1906–11 Constitutional government of Tsar and Duma

NEP

100m tons steel
200m tons grain

Tsarist autocracy

1898   RSDLP set up

1903   Lenin founded Bolshevik Party

1904–5   Russo-Japanese War

1905   Bloody Sunday. The 1905 Revolution failed. October Manifesto

1914–18   First World War

1917   February Revolution. Provisional Government

1917   October Revolution. Bolshevik Government

1918–20   Civil War. War Communism

1921   Kronstadt Rising. NEP began

1922   USSR created

50m tons steel
100m tons steel

Grain production

Steel production

Key:
- Five-year Plans
- War
- ☆ Revolution

58

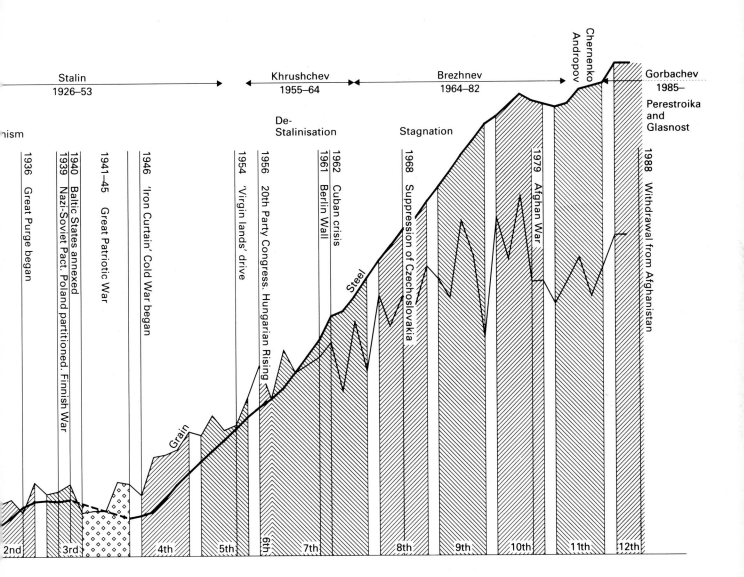

'a soviet-style manager–politician–executive, the efficient organisation man, a Communist in a grey flannel suit,' as a Western diplomat described him. A steelworker's son, Brezhnev was a schoolboy at the time of the 1917 Revolution. He trained as a surveyor and engineer, then joined the Party to further his career. As a planner with a sound practical background, he was given the job of restoring Ukrainian industry after the Second World War, then that of turning Moldavia (newly taken from Romania) into a submissive Soviet Republic. He proved firm and successful. Khrushchev thought him efficient and loyal, and brought him into the Politburo.

Brezhnev was stolid and conservative, leading a like-minded team. He wanted to preserve the Soviet system unchanged and keep the USSR at the head of the socialist world. In 1977 his new constitution added the job of President, head of state, to that of Party Secretary, and underlined the Party's role in running the USSR. His Politburo, once Khrushchev was gone, changed very little; in fact, before long most members were of pensionable age and unwilling to face change. Brezhnev remained in charge until his death at 75 in 1982. Yuri Andropov, already 68 when he succeeded, planned sweeping changes, but died just over a year later. Leadership passed briefly to the ailing septuagenarian Konstantin Chernenko, until he died early in 1985.

In two decades of stable government, Soviet output slowly improved and living standards rose. Agriculture became more productive within the framework of collectivisation, though it still lagged behind the West, and the USSR had to import vast quantities of food. Industrial development continued on a massive scale as one Five-year Plan succeeded another.

The Party remained firmly in control. The KGB, headed by Andropov from 1967 to 1982, snuffed out any hint of opposition or criticism, there were no more political murders and fewer labour camps. 'Dissidents' could be dealt with in various ways: the novelist Solzhenitsyn was expelled to the West in 1974; the nuclear scientist Sakharov was exiled to the provincial town of Gorky. Some protesters were imprisoned for anti-Soviet activities, others confined to mental hospitals. Whole groups who questioned the Party line, like Baptist Christians, were imprisoned. Newspapers, books, radio, television and films still put over the Party viewpoint, and there could be but one Party.

Nevertheless, the regime was much milder than Stalin's and dissidents made their views known through underground (samizdat) books and newspapers, circulating in typescript. An active group campaigning for human rights appeared in 1968, attempting demonstrations and making its voice heard through foreign radio stations. Because the USSR now sought friendship and trade, its rulers had to heed reactions in the non-Communist world; and there, cases of ill-treated dissidents or persecuted minorities were well publicised.

But the Soviets allowed very little freedom in eastern Europe. In 1968 Czechoslovakia's new leader, Alexander Dubcek, tried out his own brand of liberal Communism. He allowed freedom of speech, and perhaps intended free elections. Brezhnev suspected that freedom might get out of hand. Warsaw Pact troops marched in, and hard-line Communism was restored. Thereafter, Soviet leaders made sure that no satellite stepped out of line. In 1980–2 Poland was the danger, when the popular 'Solidarity' trade union movement threatened Party rule. With Soviet approval a military government took over to preserve the regime and suppress Solidarity.

Gorbachev

Under Brezhnev and his two successors the team of wise old Communists worked smoothly together, and there were no murderous power struggles. They had lived through vast changes, through tyranny, famine, world war and civil war, and a dictatorship that outdid Tsarism in repressive cruelty. Now, they could claim, Soviet citizens had jobs, food, homes, education and medical care. Yet under their ponderous regime bureaucracy, inefficienty, muddle and corruption still flourished. Russia seemed to be stagnating as it had so often in the Tsarist past.

Early in 1985 two slow-moving decades came to an end when Chernenko died, last of the old men born before the Revolution and rising to power under Stalin. He was replaced as General Secretary by Mikhail Gorbachev, just 54 and Russia's youngest ruler for fifty years.

Gorbachev promised the dynamic leadership that the USSR seemed to need. He packed the Politburo with his supporters to push forward changes. Politically, he suggested genuine elections, with more than one candidate. Economic changes were proposed, to improve productivity by ncouraging competitveness, free markets and enterprise. Further, Gorbachev favoured *glasnost*, greater freedom of discussion, so that even his own policies were criticised by those who argued thàt free competition had no place in a directed economy. Dissidents like Sakharov were released. In international affairs the new leader set out to restore friendly relations with the USA and to bring about widespread disarmament.

Gorbachev's proposed changes implied abandonment of many traditional Communist attitudes in an effort to transform the Soviet Union. It remained to be seen whether real change could take place in Russia without the need for revolutionary upheaval.

Co-existence and confrontation

In world affairs, the leaders who followed Khrushchev continued to favour co-existence. Brezhnev and President Nixon were on good terms, coming to an agreement in 1975 to hold Strategic Arms Limitation Talks (SALT). They found that co-operation paid. Both countries could spend more on relieving poverty. The USSR could rely on grain and machinery from the United States to support its industrial growth.

Unfortunately *detente* was short-lived. Late in the 1970s it gave way to renewed coolness as each side saw opportunities to gain footholds in neutral parts of the world. The USSR aided revolutionary governments in Africa and Central America; the USA overthrew pro-Soviet governments in Chile (1973) and Grenada (1983). In 1979 the Soviet Union moved into Afghanistan to support a friendly Communist leader; Brezhnev was concerned that the Islamic upsurge which had brought revolution in Iran might affect the fifty million Muslims in Soviet Central Asia. The USA condemned his action as aggression, and disagreements grew sharper as President Reagan's hard-line government took over in 1981. Not until the reforming Gorbachev took over did international tension ease.

Half a century after Stalin's revolution and seventy years after the October Revolution, the Soviet Union was one of the two powers dominating the world. Like the USA, the USSR was regarded as a source of help and guidance by some countries, with fear and suspicion by others. The superpowers represented incompatible ideologies, both rooted in the nineteenth century: liberal-democratic capitalist individualism versus Marxist-Leninist state socialism. If this was what the confrontation was about, then the bitter rivalry dividing the world must be the most dangerous of all the legacies of the October Revolution. But the clash of ideologies was in one sense simply an additional factor in Russia's traditional expansionism. The bitterness and dangers of a global power struggle owe more to the world's shrinking distances, limited resources, population pressures and ever more devastating weapons than to Russia's revolutions.

Mikhail Gorbachev (1931–   ), who became General Secretary in 1985 as a relatively young man, emphasised his new approach to leadership. He called for reforms: 'restructuring' ('perestroika') of economy and society, with 'openness' ('glasnost') about Soviet shortcomings. Another break with tradition was the visible part played by his wife, for hitherto no woman had played any part in the Communist leadership.

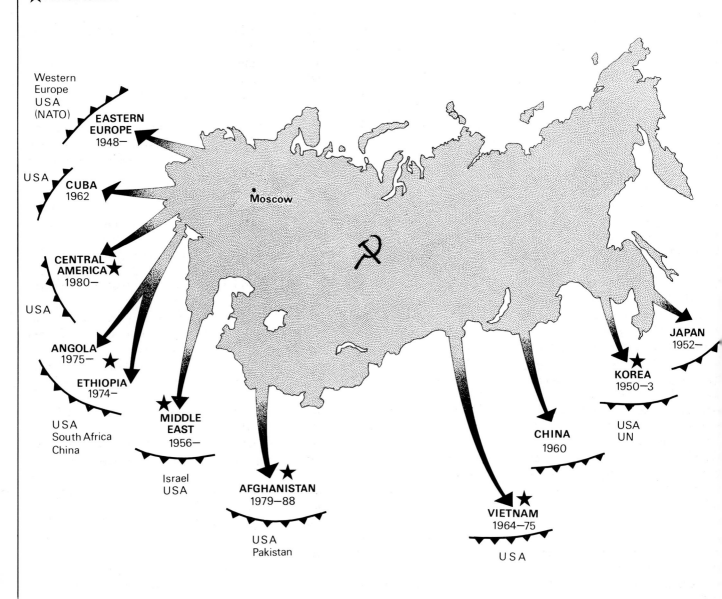

The USSR in the world since 1945

Areas of confrontation in which the USSR has
been directly or indirectly involved

★ Armed conflict

Western
Europe
USA
(NATO)

**EASTERN
EUROPE**
1948—

USA

CUBA
1962

Moscow

**CENTRAL
AMERICA** ★
1980—

USA

ANGOLA
1975— ★

ETHIOPIA
1974—

USA
South Africa
China

★
**MIDDLE
EAST**
1956—

Israel
USA

★
AFGHANISTAN
1979—88

USA
Pakistan

CHINA
1960

VIETNAM ★
1964—75

USA

KOREA ★
1950—3

USA
UN

JAPAN
1952—

Glossary

Bolsheviks 'Majority' group of *Social Democrats*, so called because Lenin gained support from most of the members left at the very end of the 1903 London conference for his forceful revolutionary policies.

Cheka government department set up in 1917 to destroy state or Party enemies. Later changed its name many times: 1922, GPU or OGPU (State Political Administration); 1934, NKVD (People's Commissariat of Internal Affairs); 1943, NKGB (People's Commissariat of State Security); 1946, MVD and MGB (Ministries of Internal Affairs and State Security); 1953, KGB (Committee for State Security).

Comintern Communist International, 1919–43, linking Communist parties in order to further world revolution under Moscow leadership.

commissar revolutionary name for a minister or official.

Duma elected 'assembly' or parliament, especially the Imperial Duma, 1906–17

glasnost 'openness', increased freedom of information and discussion allowed under Gorbachev, 1985–

intelligentsia educated people who guide opinion.

Kadets Constitutional Democrats, the liberal and progressive party in the Duma, mainly middle-class professionals, seeking the growth of parliamentary democracy.

kolkhoz 'collective farm', sharing work and returns.

Kremlin the old fortress-palace in Moscow which became the heart of Communist rule.

kulaks 'fists' or tight-fisted farmers who built up their own farms, often at the expense of the rest of the village.

Land Captain magistrate appointed from 1889 to supervise a village.

Mensheviks 'Minority' group of Social Democrats at the close of the 1903 conference, who expected an inevitable socialist revolution without violence.

mir the village community acting together.

Narodnaia Volia 'People's Will,' Narodnik group of the 1880s, using terrorist methods.

Narodniks 'Populists', sympathisers with the common people, 1860s on, who hoped to win political rights for peasants.

NEP New Economic Policy, the Soviet programme 1921–8, to restore the economy by allowing some private enterprise.

Octobrists Conservatives in the Duma, mainly country gentry and businessmen who based their policies on the October Manifesto of 1905.

Okhrana Tsarist political police, often using secret agents to detect and crush treasonable activity.

pogrom organised violent attack on a minority group, especially Jews.

Politburo the small 'Policy Committee' heading the Bolshevik Party in 1917, revived in 1919, and acting as the real government of the USSR ever since (though known as the Praesidium 1952–66).

Pravda 'Truth', the Bolshevik/Communist newspaper publishing the Party viewpoint.

Romanov the family ruling the Russian Empire 1613–1917.

rouble standard unit of currency; before 1914 a silver coin (or paper note) worth about 2 shillings, one-tenth of a British pound or one-half of a US dollar.

samizdat 'self-publishing' the unofficial underground press in the USSR.

Social Democrats *(SDs)* Marxists who formed the Russian Social Democratic Labour Party in 1898 to transform Russia into a Marxist workers', or socialist, state.

Socialist Revolutionaries *(SRs)* from the non-Marxist Socialist Revolutionary Party formed in 1901 to win political power for the peasant masses.

Sovnarkom 'Council of People's Commissars', the USSR's central government, 1917–46.

soviet elected committee representing workers, peasants or soldiers; the Supreme Soviet is the central assembly of the USSR.

Trudoviks members of the *Trudovaia* (labour) *Gruppa* in the Duma, mainly *SRs*.

USSR the Union of Soviet Socialist Republics, set up in 1922.

War Communism Soviet government policy 1918–21, when all production was controlled for the war effort.

zemstvo elected local or provincial council.

Index